TRUE
MONSTER
STORIES

TRUE MONSTER STORIES

Terry Deary

Hippo Books
Scholastic Children's Books
London

Scholastic Children's Books,
Scholastic Publications Ltd,
7-9 Pratt Street, London NW1 0AE, UK

Scholastic Inc.,
730 Broadway, New York, NY 10003, USA

Scholastic Canada Ltd,
123 Newkirk Road, Richmond Hill,
Ontario, Canada L4C 3G5

Ashton Scholastic Pty Ltd,
P O Box 579, Gosford, New South Wales,
Australia

Ashton Scholastic Ltd,
Private Bag 1, Penrose, Auckland,
New Zealand

ISBN 0 590 55042 X

Typeset by Contour Typesetters, Southall, London
Made and printed by Cox and Wyman, Reading

CONTENTS

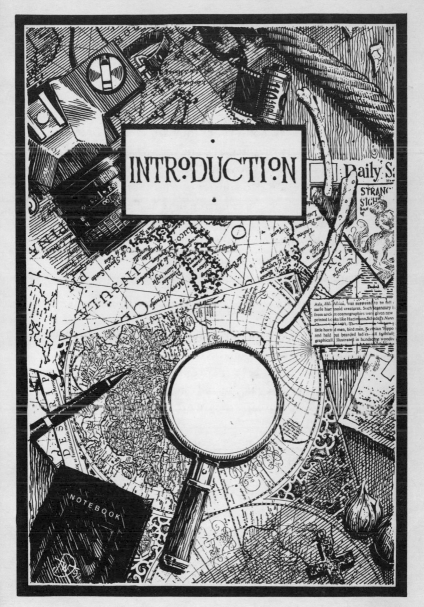

INTRODUCTION

Monsters! Monsters! Monsters!

People have been telling stories about monsters ever since they could tell stories. They're the things that we meet in nightmares. They scare the life out of us. We love them!

What is a 'monster'? A dictionary will tell you it's a misshapen animal. Sometimes monsters are huge, like the creature in Loch Ness. Sometimes they are small, like the little vampire bat. Usually they are evil and out to harm humans. But what we really want to know is, "Are they real?"

Here is a collection of monster stories. Some from distant times and distant places. Some from here and now. Somebody, somewhere, at some time swore that each one was true. You have to make up your own mind.

All I can do is give you this clue. There are three explanations for monster stories: fibs, foolishness and facts.

Fibs

People tell lies. Many people have told monster fibs about monsters; amazing stories.

There are stories that help them explain something – like the girl who let her herd of yak die and claimed they were attacked by a giant ape man. Perhaps they were . . . but why did the ape man not attack her?

There are stories that make people sit up and take notice of you – like the man who read about the monster Bigfoot in America and decided to tell the world about the time he was kidnapped by a family of them. Perhaps he was . . . but why did he wait thirty years to tell his sensational tale?

There are stories that make you money – "Roll up, roll up! For just one dollar see the fearsome Hodag, with huge claws, bulging eyes, large horns and a line of spikes down its back!" But the Hodag was a stuffed fake of 1890s United States. So was the Fur-Bearing Trout, the Jackalope (a rabbit with antlers), the Jenny Haniver (a stuffed ray-fish moulded into a dragon shape) and many more. The great American showman, P. T. Barnum, once said of people who believe anything, "There's one born every minute." And there were thousands of what he called "suckers" ready to pay good money to see a dead, shrivelled fish. Fakes! Fibs!

Foolishness

Anyone can make a mistake. Honest, clever people make mistakes. Honest, clever people make fools of themselves over monsters.

If you're in the dark and scared, then a bat becomes a vampire and a scarecrow becomes a giant.

Two hundred years ago clever people heard tales of a monster that was as tall as a tree. It was shaped like a camel and was spotted like a leopard. They hadn't seen it, but they gave it a name: the camel-leopard. It was a monster from your worst nightmares. Would you like to meet one? Actually, you probably have. Eventually one was caught and brought into a zoo. It was given a new name – giraffe!

Not a monster and not a fib, just an honest mistake. Foolishness!

Facts

Somewhere out there in the natural world there are things we don't understand. We've heard the fibs and the foolishness of them and we're not sure if we should believe them. But if we look hard enough we can sometimes see the truth behind the stories.

Travellers back from Africa said they had seen unicorns. The *fact* is there are one-horned creatures roaming the plains. The *fact* is we call them rhinoceros.

Sailors home from the sea described mermaids. The *fact* is there are creatures called manatee which look almost human with fishy tails. Is that what they had seen?

In northern Europe people told tales of the huge Kraken. Had they seen giant squid?

Even when there are no facts to explain a monster, you have to remember the earth is very large and very old. Just because we haven't found the body or bones of a Yeti doesn't mean that it doesn't exist. There must still be things out there that we can't explain as fibs or foolishness.

They are the real monsters we are searching for.

Can you sort out the fact from the fiction? Can you find the truth about monsters in these True Monster Stories?

Enjoy finding out.

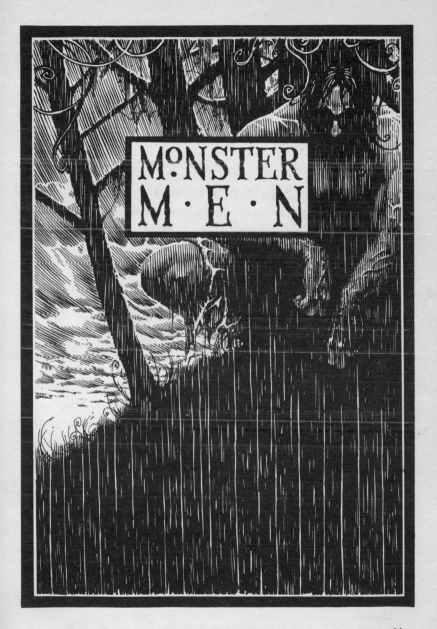

Of all the monsters, the ones that look human and act inhumanly are the most fearsome. They are the stuff of legends. The Greeks had the one-eyed, flesh-eating, giant Cyclops. They had the beautiful Siren women who lured sailors to their deaths. One of the oldest poems in the English language describes an encounter between a hero, Beowulf, and a dreadful giant, Grendel:

> From the stretching moors, from the misty hollows,
> Grendel came creeping
> To feast his fill on the flesh of men.

> The demon delayed not, but quickly clutched,
> Tore men to pieces, bit through the bones,
> Gulped the blood and gobbled the flesh,
> Greedily gorged on the lifeless corpses.

> Then the fiend stepped nearer
> But Beowulf grappled and gripped him hard.
> Sinews snapped and bone-joints broke
> And Beowulf gained the glory of battle.

Through the ages every country has had its tales of wild men. Some were fierce and some were timid but most lived alone in forests and were very strong. They needed to be for the forests were full of wolves and bears.

There were legends about wild children being brought up by wolves and growing up as wolves. That story goes back as far as Ancient Rome. The two men who founded Rome, Romulus and Remus, were said to have been raised by a wolf after their cruel uncle left them in the wilds to die. Impossible? Well, a missionary in Bengal in the early 1900s described how he came across two such girls aged about five. The villagers rescued them from a mother wolf and he took them to an orphanage. He called them Amala, who died after just a year, and Kamala who survived a further nine years and learned to act like a human.

There was also a boy found in the jungle of Sri Lanka in 1973 who had been raised by monkeys. He could run on all fours but not stand straight or speak. There are photographs of the boy to prove that story. So wild humans are *possible* . . . and if they are evil as well as wild then they become True Monsters.

Judge each story for yourself and decide whether you think it is true.

The Wild Man of Wales

Megan was a hard woman. It was a hard life on the mountain farm. You had to be tough to survive.

She stood at the door of her cottage and watched the sun slip down behind the mountains. "Rhiannon!" she called sharply. "Carys!" It was too late for her daughters to be out, especially after what she'd heard in the chapel yesterday.

The two girls tumbled, breathless, round the farmyard wall, eyes shining and excited.

"Oh, Ma!" Rhiannon, the elder one, gasped. "You should hear what Tegwyn's been saying down in the village."

"So that's where you've been. Gossiping, is it?" their mother said harshly.

"Sorry, Ma," Carys said. "Were you worried about us?"

"Worried?" the woman snorted. "Why would I be worried?"

"In case the wild man got us," Rhiannon said breathlessly.

Her mother pushed a bowl of soup across the table towards the child. "More scared that you would get the wild man," she said and her hard mouth turned up a little at the corners.

"It's not funny, Ma!" Carys said. "Tegwyn said there was a robbery at Penlan Farm on Saturday and Aberdyfi Farm last night. He's working his way up the valley, Ma." Her bright eyes widened and her voice dropped. "They reckon it's our turn next."

"You don't want to go listening to all that wild man nonsense. I'm ashamed that Tegwyn Morris would go filling your head with such stuff!"

"It's not nonsense," Rhiannon urged. "They set a trap for him at Aberdyfi last night. They *saw* him! He had hardly any clothes, just skins they say. And he had long red shaggy hair! They saw him in the moonlight going into the barn. Dropped a net over him!"

The girl bent her head to sip the hot soup while her sister went on with the story. "But he tore his way out of it with his bare hands, Ma. He's stronger than Dyfed Evans's bull, they reckon."

Megan's eyes narrowed. She spoke quietly. "Finish that soup. Then I want you to wash, brush your hair and say your prayers, you understand?"

"Yes, Ma," the girls murmured.

"Especially your prayers. Pray your dad gets home safe from market tomorrow eh?"

"Yes, Ma."

"And forget about wild men. If you say your prayers there's nothing bad can get you – not by day and not by night. I don't want you losing any beauty sleep over it. See?"

The girls nodded and finished their meal in silence, kissed their mother and said goodnight.

Megan sat in the flickering shadows of the oil-lamp till the only sound from the girls' room was their soft snoring. She stood up and began to move briskly. First she bolted the door carefully and checked that every window was shuttered. She blew out the lamp and moved into the kitchen.

Carefully she opened the window shutter, letting the ice-bright moonlight flow over the stone-flagged floor. Something glinted in the log basket. She picked it up and returned to the window where she sat on a stool like a cat at a mouse-hole.

The moon rose higher and brighter. The only sounds were the owls in the valley and a late curlew that stirred from its sleep. The woman nodded in her chair as the hours slid past.

Then came a sound, soft as a cat's footstep.

Megan stiffened and strained her eyes. Something in the shadows of the barn was moving. A gentle rattle at the barn door . . . but that was firmly shut. Nothing there. Her hand clutched the thing from the log basket. The other hand reached out and touched the big black Bible on the table.

"Behold, I come as a thief," she murmured, remembering the chapel lessons from her childhood.

One shadow, edged with silver, moved away from the barn and into the moonlight shining on the cobbled yard. A man. A huge and almost shapeless bundle of rags. He was drawn to the open shutter like a moth to a candle flame. Megan froze in the shadow and shrank against the wall.

She could hear his harsh breathing, smell the stench from his animal clothes and finally, see the filthy clawed hand reaching through the open window. Megan's mouth was dry. But her hand was wet with sweat where it was wrapped around the axe from the log basket. She swept the axe down as expertly as she did when she was splitting logs. There was a wail like a wounded dog as the stranger tumbled back out of the window . . . and the hand jumped onto the kitchen floor.

Megan breathed out for the first time in minutes. She watched the sobbing creature stagger across the yard and into the valley. With a shaking hand she lit the lamp and turned the Bible to her favourite chapter. "Resist the devil and he will flee from you," she said.

She stayed awake all that night, reading. As the first light turned the sky slate grey she took the severed hand in a cloth and wrapped herself in a shawl. She knew her children would be safe now.

Megan hurried down to the village and found tired men gathering at the market cross. "Sorry, Megan, no sign of the wild man," Tegwyn Evans said.

But Megan opened the cloth and showed the men. "I think if you follow the trail of blood from my house you will find him."

As the sun rose they found the trail and followed it to a cave hidden behind a waterfall. But the wild man was gone. He never returned to Nanhrynan. Yet, still today, that place is called the Cave of Owen Langoch – the Cave of the Red-haired man.

But that wild man was no match for a caring mother.

Monster Men – FACT FILE

1. The wild man legend almost killed the king of France. In 1392 Charles VI went to a carnival with friends. They dressed as the legendary wild men with masks of tar and paper. Someone took a torch to peer more closely at the dancers and the costumes burst into flames. Charles's mother saved him by smothering him with a cloak. His four friends died.

2. A Scottish mountain has its own giant. This mountain, Ben MacDhui in the Cairngorms, has the Big Grey Man. Many very experienced climbers claim to have seen him. The huge, grey figure has feet like a bird of prey and pointed ears. It must be difficult to see them though – they are about 6 metres off the ground!

3. Not all wild men were reported to be hairy. Some were covered with leaves or moss. They were, naturally enough, known as Green Men. Groups of actors, called Mummers, still dress up as Green Men to perform in country festivals.

4. In the Alps there is a legend of a wild woman. She can charm men in spite of her ugliness. She has tremendous strength and has a taste for eating children! Could this be the source of the witch in the Hansel and Gretel story?

5.   The tallest recorded man was Robert Pershing Wadlow who was born in the United States in 1918. He was 2.72 metres tall, but soon outgrew his strength and died at the age of 22.

6.   In the Bible there is a description of King Nebuchadnezzar who "was driven from men and did eat grass like an ox. His body was wet with the dew of heaven till his hair grew like eagles' feathers and his nails like birds' claws."

7.   If Goliath was really 6 cubits tall, as the Bible story says, then he would measure 2.9 metres. The earliest Greek version of the Bible says he was 4 Greek cubits – 2.08 metres – which is much more likely.

8.   Wild men are said to have appeared as wolves (usually called werewolves), as leopards (in Africa in the 1930s) and even as owls. At the time of the sighting of the sea monster Morgawr in Cornwall, a sixteen-year-old girl swore she saw "a monster like a devil flying up through the trees near old Mawnan church." The girl and her friend admitted that they thought it was someone dressed up in an owl costume for a joke. But when the man took off and flew into a tree they were pretty surprised.

9.   In England in the 1200s a wild man was caught by fishermen in the North Sea. A monk at that time wrote that the man was very strong and lived on raw fish.

Apart from being unusually hairy he was like a human in every way – he wasn't a merman. After a few months his captors tired of him and he escaped, never to be seen again.

10.   Just as Yeti, Yowie and Bigfoot are believed to be descendants of the ancient Gigantopithecus ape, so some people believe that wild men are remnants of the prehistoric Neanderthal man.

Some monster men are fakes, not true monsters or unknown creatures at all but men with a cruelly twisted sense of humour. Perhaps one such man roamed the streets of Victorian London, terrorising women fifty years before the famous Jack the Ripper appeared on the scene.

Perhaps it was all a wicked joke. At the time there was no mystery about the monster. It seemed that everyone knew who he was. But he was never caught in the act and he was too well known and important a person to be arrested just on rumours.

Yet this mystery remains. If he was a normal human with a nasty sense of humour, where did he get the power to escape capture by leaping over walls and fences where no policeman could ever follow? For that was how he got his name . . .

Spring-Heeled Jack

18 February 1838
Green Dragon Alley was cold and Green Dragon Alley was dark. But on that night Green Dragon Alley was the lair of something more fearful than a dragon.

The stinking streets of London were no place for two young ladies that night. Anyone with any sense was at home sitting in front of a blazing coal fire. The smoke from the fires thickened the dark city air. But Lucy and Margaret Scales were out in the dank and deserted streets. They lifted their skirts to step through the mixture of mud and rubbish. They shivered in their shawls, put their heads down and hurried home.

"We shouldn't have left it so late!" Margaret moaned.

"Don't be silly," Lucy sighed. "We'll be safe if we stay together." But Lucy didn't sound too sure of that.

Margaret clung to the sleeve of her sister's dress and groaned again. "I think my feet are going to drop off with tiredness."

"No they are not!" her sister said firmly. "Just stand here a while and rest," she ordered and leaned against a street lamp.

"Read the newspaper to me again," Margaret whispered.

Lucy pulled out the torn page from her purse. She held it up to catch the flickering orange light. "It says, '*Peckham Prowler Puzzles Police*' . . ."

"Go on," Margaret urged.

Her sister read on. " 'Last night the Lord Mayor of London, Sir John Cowan, made a sensational statement to the gentlemen of the press at Mansion House. Sir John claimed that he had received a letter signed *A Peckham Resident*. The letter claimed that a person of high rank had made a bet that he would disguise himself and scare thirty people to death . . .' "

"Ohh!" Margaret whimpered. "Just the thought of it is scaring me to death."

Lucy went on, " 'He has already succeeded in frightening seven ladies out of their senses. Two of the ladies are not likely to recover. The writer asked, what were the police going to do about the man? The mayor announced that the police would be putting every effort into catching this deranged man. They were puzzled because he has appeared in so many disguises. He has appeared as a white bull, as a bear, and as a baboon. He has been seen wearing shining armour and in Hackney as a lamplighter who walked on his hands and carried his ladders between his feet. Sir John said that extra police will patrol the area until this evil man is caught.' "

Margaret gave a small cry. "He could be anywhere."

"Well, he's not here," Lucy snapped. "Come on, Margaret. We're almost at Green Dragon Alley then we're home. Do you feel well enough?"

"No–o. I wish we hadn't gone to see George tonight."

"We always go to see George on Wednesday evenings – and no mad man is going to stop me," said Lucy. "Anyway, since the mayor made that speech no one has seen this Peckham

Prowler . . . and that's five or six weeks ago now. Take my word for it, Margaret, we're safe."

"Just read that last piece," her sister said.

Lucy peered at the paper and said, " 'Police claim their attempts to catch the man have only failed because the man has such power to leap to great heights. It is believed that he must have springs in his boots. The terrified people of London have already given this monster a name – they call him Spring-Heeled Jack!' "

"Spring-Heeled Jack!" Margaret breathed. "I think I'll stay here till a policeman comes."

"Don't be so stupid. You'll freeze to death."

"I don't care!"

"Once we're past Green Dragon Alley we're safe!"

"I'm not moving till I see a policeman."

"Then you can stay here until Spring-Heeled Jack comes and gets you!" her sister said and walked off into the mist.

"Don't leave me!" Margaret squeaked and hurried after Lucy who had already reached the corner of Green Dragon Alley. But Margaret slithered on the slimy cobbles and stumbled onto her knees.

Margaret was never able to remember very clearly what happened next. It was too quick . . . and too incredible.

Lucy had stopped on the corner of Green Dragon Alley to wait for Margaret. Suddenly a dark shadow leapt out from the alley and stood behind Lucy. Margaret tried to scream but no sound came from her frightened throat. Lucy turned slowly and came face to face with the monstrous man.

As Margaret watched, the man leaned forward and breathed a gust of fire into his victim's face.

The fog swallowed the sound as Lucy fell in a dead faint. It swallowed too the dark, leaping figure with the bulging eyes.

Spring-Heeled Jack had left the poor people of Peckham in

peace for five weeks. But now he was back with a new and nasty trick. For, when Margaret reached her sister, Lucy's pale face was scorched and her hair singed.

From far away, through the fog, there came a cackle of evil laughter.

20 February 1838

Jane Alsop ran to the front door of her parents' house. Someone was ringing the bell wildly.

She threw open the door and at first saw no one in the dim street. Then a man called to her from the shadows of the pavement, "For God's sake, bring a light! I am a policeman. We have just caught Spring-Heeled Jack in the lane!"

The girl hurried to obey and returned to the door a few seconds later with a candle.

As she handed it to the 'policeman' he threw off his huge cloak. He appeared to be wearing a tight-fitting helmet on his head, and a shiny, white suit. His eyes bulged and sparkled in the light of a candle.

Suddenly he breathed across the candle. A ball of flame burst into Jane's face. As she staggered back, half blinded, he clutched at her with claws like a bird of prey and ripped her dress.

Jane's screams brought her sisters, Mary and Sarah, running. Sarah tore Jane from the monster's grasp, pulled her back into the house and managed to slam the door.

Spring-Heeled Jack had carried out his most vicious and daring raid yet. The young women of London were not safe even in their own homes. He was the worst kind of monster.

Spring-Heeled Jack – FACT FILE

1.   Spring-Heeled Jack became a legend in his own time. He became the popular hero (or villain) of short thriller stories known as 'penny dreadfuls'. The character also appeared in popular theatre shows of the time.

2.   A lot of fiction was written about him. In time he turned from being a villain to being a kind of super-hero. The result was that over the years people tended to forget he really existed. Some writers have claimed that he was just a legend created by servants to explain accidents and thefts in the home.

3.   Attacks by Spring-Heeled Jack were reported, on and off, for the next 66 years. By the last one in 1904 the original Jack must have been 80 or 90 years old! He was also sighted in many parts of the country. It is clear that there were many copy-cat Jacks.

4.   Some people suggested that Jack was a mad circus fire-eater. Others said he was a kangaroo dressed up by a lunatic animal trainer.

5.   The most believable suggestion was that Jack was in fact the young Lord Waterford who would have been about 27 or 28 at the time of the first attacks. The clues pointing to him are:
    Lord Waterford was a well-known practical joker; he had bulging eyes;

Spring-Heeled Jack had the letter 'W' on the front of his white suit;

Lord Waterford was always in London at the time of Spring-Heeled Jack's activities;

Lord Waterford was a great athlete, quite capable of out-running and out-jumping police;

he was noted for his cruelty to people and animals.

6.   Lord Waterford settled down to a quiet married life in 1842, by which time the attacks had stopped. When they started again they were obviously the work of someone else.

7.   In 1845 a Spring-Heeled Jack caused his first death. Thirteen-year-old Maria Davis was cornered by a fire-breathing man and thrown into a muddy ditch where she slowly drowned.

8.   A Spring-Heeled Jack was caught in 1845. He was leaping over hedges and walls with shrieks and groans in West London. It turned out to be a young butcher from Brentford. He was too young to have been the attacker in 1838.

9.   In 1877 a Spring-Heeled Jack appeared, breathing fire, at an army barracks in Aldershot. The guard fired at him and scared him off but didn't hurt him. Jack gained the reputation for being magically shielded from bullets. In fact the guard had fired blanks.

10.   In 1944 a similar character appeared in Mattoon Town, Illinois. He wore a tight-fitting suit and a gas mask. People who saw him standing outside their open bedroom window became ill the next day. They claimed the Mad Gasser of Mattoon was spraying deadly fumes into the air. Who he was, where he came from and where he went remains a mystery.

MONSTER BIRDS

Monsters that swoop down from the skies and carry off their victims are every bit as horrifying as the ones that lurk in the woods and the caves of earth, or the dark depths of lakes and oceans. Since the days of the Pterodactyls, death has hovered in the skies. The flying dinosaurs are long dead, but some of their descendants, the birds, are still sometimes believed to be a threat to humans . . . especially children . . .

The Thunderbird

An old man looked over the parched Missouri plains. His skin was dry and wrinkled as parchment and his eyes glinted watery blue in the sunlight. Sad eyes. Eyes that had seen a monster and would never forget.

He sat in the afternoon sun, still as death, the old eyes fixed on the faded blue sky.

"Good day!" a young hiker called, uncertainly. He had thick walking boots, and a large back pack. Around his neck he carried expensive binoculars.

After a few moments the old man turned his gaze towards the hiker and nodded in greeting.

"Nice day," the young man grinned.

The old man thought about it for a moment. Then he jerked his head forward on his scrawny neck and hissed, "Not much cover out there on the plain!"

The hiker stepped back. "No-o," he agreed. "But what would you want cover for?"

The old man narrowed his eyes and murmured, "From the bird."

The young man gave a small sigh and dropped his pack on the dusty earth. He tapped his binoculars. "I'm interested in bird-watching too," he grinned. "I'm Al . . . Al Duncan." He stretched out a hand.

"Edward Colgin," the old man grunted and shook hands with a fierce grip that made the hiker's eyes water.

"You want to have a look through my binoculars?" Al offered.

"I may look old but my eyes are sharper than a timber-wolf's tooth," Edward sniffed.

"Cost fifty dollars," the young man boasted. "Made in Germany! You'll see your birds much clearer with these," he offered again.

Old Edward's face hardened. "I won't need no fancy eyeglasses for the bird I'm waiting for. It's big enough."

"Ah, you're looking for eagles, are you? I heard there were plenty round here."

Edward shook his head slowly. "Not eagles. Bigger than that."

Al scratched his head. "Won't get anything bigger than an eagle in Missouri," he shrugged.

Edward Colgin turned on him fiercely. "Oh, you know that, do you? You know that for a fact?"

"Well . . ."

"Because I happen to know that there is a bigger bird. Bigger than any bird you've ever seen."

Al laughed nervously. "What sort of bird's that, Mr Colgin?"

The old man stared hard at the sky. "The Thunderbird."

The young hiker gasped. "That's an Indian legend . . . just a story. We learned it at school."

"You did, did you?" Edward said quietly.

"Yeah! It was the Illini tribe, wasn't it? They called it 'the-bird-that-eats-humans" – the *piasa*. But that was a hundred years ago. Teacher used to tell us how Ouatogo killed it."

"He did, did he?" the old man snorted.

"Yes," Al went on eagerly. "He stood out in the open and

waited for the *piasa* to attack. But twenty of his warriors were hiding in the rocks. As the bird swooped on Ouatogo they killed it with their arrows." The hiker chuckled. "So even if you believe the legend, the creature was killed."

"Is that a fact?" Edward grunted sourly. He stared back into the glare of the autumn sky and said, "Then I'll tell you another story. But this story just happens to be true. It happened just fifty years ago – back in 1878 in Tippah County. That's Tippah County on the other side of the river, see it?"

Al sank down onto his back pack and nodded.

"The farmers had lost a lot of stock that autumn. The settlers had driven the wildlife off the plains. The birds of prey had nothing left to catch. So they turned on the farm animals. Those farmers complained about the pigs and the sheep they were losing – reckoned it was eagles. But they were wrong."

"But how do you know, Mr Colgin?" Al insisted.

The old man didn't seem to hear the question. He was looking at the blank, blue sky and seeing pictures from fifty years before. "Of course, no one believed the birds could harm people. An eagle couldn't attack a human, could it? So they got careless. It was a Thursday. Recess. The school teacher let the kids out into the field to play then went back in to have a coffee. The next thing he knew there were screams from the field. He dashed out in time to see a huge bird rising into the air . . . with an eight-year-old boy in his claws." Edward Colgin swallowed hard and his sharp eyes seemed to cloud for a few moments. "Poor little Jemmie Kenney."

The young hiker stretched out a hand and laid it on the old man's arm. "An eagle?"

The old man shook his head and sniffed. "Too big. Two or even three times the size of an eagle."

"A Thunderbird?"

"I can still hear the screams of poor little Jemmie," Edward said hoarsely. "Struggled so hard the bird had to drop him . . . dropped him practically at my feet."

"Dead?"

The old man snorted. A question too stupid to deserve an answer.

"You were there, Mr Colgin?"

"I was the teacher. I was to blame. I let the Thunderbird kill Jemmie Kenney."

"You can't say that, Mr Colgin."

"The rest of Tippah County did," the teacher said bitterly. "Lost my job. Had to turn to keeping pigs. The Thunderbird killed part of me when he killed Jemmie Kenney," he said.

Al shook his head. "You didn't ought to blame yourself, Mr Colgin. Nothing you can do about it now."

The old man's thin lips turned up in a grim smile. "Oh, no? Aren't you forgetting that story about old Ouatogo?"

"You mean that's why you're sitting out here? Bait? Waiting for the Thunderbird to attack again?" Al cried. He didn't believe it. Still he glanced nervously up into the empty sky . . . the almost empty sky. High above a small dot circled.

Al jumped to his feet and fumbled with his binoculars. His trembling hands couldn't hold them steady and they fell to the ground. But he didn't need them now. For the dot was falling towards them and growing bigger every second. Al began to back away down the dusty trail. "But Mr Colgin . . . Ouatogo had twenty warriors hiding in the rocks!"

The old man sat calm as the rocks on the hillside. The bird cast a shadow over the path. Edward Colgin slid a hand inside his shirt and gently pulled out a huge Colt pistol. "Fifty years, I've waited, Jemmie, fifty years!"

The young man screamed and the old man laughed as a huge bird began to fill the sky above his head . . .

Monster Birds – FACT FILE

1.   In 1878 Jemmie Kenney was indeed snatched by a huge bird while his teacher looked on helplessly. But scientists have claimed that an eagle could lift nothing larger than a fawn or young goat. So what sort of bird took Jemmie?

2.   The largest known living bird is the Wandering Albatross with a wingspan of 3.3 metres, but that was only ever seen in the southern oceans. An Arctic expedition claimed to have measured a Wandering Albatross at 4. 22 metres but this was not confirmed.

3.   The largest known extinct bird is the Terahorn, which had a truly monstrous 7.5-metre wingspan. Fossils have been found in the Southern United States (where Jemmie was snatched) – but it died out at least 10 000 years ago . . . didn't it?

4.   Some native American Indians claim they still see the Thunderbird today. They describe it as bigger than an aeroplane. The Illini tribe says it has horns and red eyes. The Haida tribe believes that the Thunderbird is a form of human ghost.

5.   After the death of Jemmie Kenney there were regular reports of giant birds in the United States. They have also been blamed for some mysterious disappearances. Some sightings say the birds had a wingspan of over 5 metres.

6.   Giant birds have been reported in Europe too. Marie Delex was taken by a large bird in 1838 in Switzerland. Her body was found a couple of months later. As a small five-year-old it's believable. But 100 years later, Svanhild Hantvigsen claimed that as a three-year-old in Norway she was taken to an eagle's nest . . . and she lived to tell the tale! That story is harder to believe.

7.   In 1976 there was a series of reported attacks in Texas by a huge winged creature. The witnesses swore it was a Pteranodon. These flying reptiles are supposed to have become extinct 64 million years ago. Explanations are:

The witnesses saw rare local birds;

Pteranodons survived, unknown to humans;

there was a time warp in that place and witnesses had glimpses of prehistoric skies.

8.   Reports of creatures that are half-human, half-bird are even more common than sightings of prehistoric creatures. In Point Pleasant, West Virginia in 1966 a bat-winged man making a squeaking noise like a large mouse chased a car which was doing 100 miles per hour (160 kph). The creature became known as Mothman. Several sightings that year established that he was 1.5 to 2 metres tall, grey-brown in colour and headless. He had a pair of glowing, red eyes where his shoulders should be and a wingspan of about 3 metres.

9.   Not many known birds of prey measure up to the descriptions of monster birds. The Andean Condor of South America can weigh 11.3 kg and a Californian Condor is claimed to have reached 14.1 kg. Could such a bird carry a human child weighing more than itself? In October 1991 in Cairns, Australia, a six-year-old girl was lifted 30 metres into the air . . . on the end of a kite! She fell from about 15 metres and luckily survived.

10.   The biggest bird of legend was the Roc which featured in the story of Sinbad. It fed elephants to its young. When Sinbad annoyed it the Roc picked up a boulder, dropped it on one of Sinbad's ships and sank it. Impossible? Yes, but the Arabian sailors probably did come across the real live Elephant Bird when they sailed to Madagascar. It looked like an ostrich but laid eggs six times the size of ostrich's eggs – that's about 148 times the size of a chicken's egg. Sadly it became extinct about 500 years ago.

THE
LOCHNESS
MONSTER

The Loch Ness Monster is probably the most famous monster in the world today. Thousands of people have reported it – no one has yet proved it exists. Look at these two stories and some of the facts, then make up your own mind . . .

The Legend

The day was hot and getting hotter. The monks trudged onwards, tired and thirsty, their rough wool robes growing warm and itchy. One young monk looked up towards the purple Scottish mountain shimmering in the heat. Still five weary miles to go. Then he looked towards the cool, deep water of the lake the locals called Loch Ness.

The monk licked his dry lips and hurried forward to where the leader strode along the shoreline. "Father Columba! Father Columba!" he panted.

The old monk turned and frowned. "Yes, my son?"

"Could we . . . could I stop for a swim?" he asked nervously.

Father Columba looked at him for a long while, then his stern face softened. "Of course, Edwin. It will do us all good to rest."

Edwin put down his bundle, pulled the rope from his waist and tugged the heavy habit over his head. Even in this heat the wind off the loch was cool and made him shudder. The water was dark brown with the peat washed down by the mountain stream. Suddenly it looked unfriendly.

But the other monks were sitting by the edge of the water soaking their dusty feet and urging Edwin on.

"What's the matter?" one called. "Scared the Kelpie's going to get you?"

"The what?" Edwin asked nervously.

"The Kelpie," Father Columba nodded. "They say the natives worship a water spirit called a Kelpie. One lives in every lake in this land."

"We Christians don't believe such things!" the young monk laughed, uncertain. Then he asked, "What sort of water spirit?"

"A monster," one monk teased. "A huge and hungry monster. He'd swallow you in one bite then spit out the bones."

"There's no such thing," Edwin said.

The other monk shrugged and asked, "Then why not dive in?"

So, to save his pride, young Edwin had to walk forward into the dark water. It was freezing, so cold it numbed his skin first

then made it tingle. His teeth chattered. The water came up to his waist. He dipped till his shoulders went under the water. He gasped with the shock, then pushed forward into a slow swimming stroke. The monks on the pebbled beach gave an encouraging cheer. He rolled onto his back to wave at them.

Suddenly the cheers turned to cries of horror. Edwin saw them stare in wonder at some point high above his head. He turned and saw it.

The monster towered out of the water twice as high as a man. It had a head like a snake and a gaping mouth. The skin was dark as wet leather. But worst were the eyes: small and evil and looking straight at him.

Edwin struggled to turn but the weed seemed to catch at his feet and drag him back. The monster slid silently forward and opened its lipless mouth further. The young monk flapped at the water like a wounded duck. The other monks had backed away from the water's edge and some fell on their knees to pray.

But Father Columba stepped forward and clutched the wooden cross he wore around his neck. Raising the wooden cross towards the creature he ordered it back to its home in hell where it belonged.

Edwin heard the water bubble and gurgle like a boiling pot as the monster sank. The fear made him faint and the water sucked at him. His limp body slipped below the water. By the time the frightened monks had dragged his body from the freezing water it was too late.

"Dead," an old monk muttered.

On the slopes above Loch Ness some local people gathered. They'd seen Father Columba drive the monster off. Still, the creature's power was great enough to kill this Christian newcomer. Columba knew he had to act or all the monks' good work would be of no use.

He knelt down and laid a hand upon young Edwin's body as he said an urgent prayer. The natives shook their heads in wonder. Edwin coughed, he groaned, he sat up and clung to old Columba.

The story of the miracle was written down a hundred long years later. It is the first report in writing that we have about a creature in the loch. Columba found his place in history and became a saint.

Yet it is the monster that is better remembered. Known and wondered at all around the world. Known today by everyone as the famous Loch Ness Monster.

The Loch Ness Monster was forgotten for hundreds of years. Then in 1933, a new road was built around the loch. New views of it had been opened up to many more people. If the monster was in the habit of popping up for a look at the world then it was just a matter of time before it would be seen, and photographed . . . by someone. That first someone was Mr Hugh Gray. On his way home from church on 13 November 1933 he saw a disturbance in the loch and took five photographs. They weren't clear photographs. They didn't prove a thing. But they started off the monster hunt that's been going on ever since.

People began to 'remember' seeing a monster thirty or fifty years before. They said they hadn't reported it at the time for fear of being laughed at. Others retold stories of 'sightings' over the centuries right back to Saint Columba's adventure.

That was when the monster hunters came to Loch Ness. Some of the hunters may have been out for a bit of fun. But others took the monster – and their hunting skills – very seriously.

Who in the world was the best person to seek and capture a huge, wild creature? A big game hunter, of course. Someone skilled in tracking and snaring wildlife in Africa. If he could capture rhinos and elephants in Africa then surely he could capture this thing in a Scottish loch, couldn't he?

The great day arrived when the Big Game Hunter moved into the lakeside hotel. He was met by reporters after a good story. He was keenly watched by locals who were interested in seeing the great man . . . and by someone who was interested in a little mischievous fun . . .

The Monster Hunter

"Mr Wetherall! Mr Wetherall!" a girl cried. "I'm from the *Daily Mail*. I'm Sally Jarvis. Can we talk about your expedition?"

Mr Wetherall looked down his fine nose at the eager girl. "I don't like interviews," he said coldly.

Sally blinked. "But, Mr Wetherall, my newspaper is paying all your expenses to come here. Surely part of the deal is that you let us know what's happening?"

The explorer sighed, settled on a stool at the hotel bar and sniffed, "Oh, very well. Just this once."

Sally was upset to discover that reporters from the other newspapers had their notepads at the ready. Ready to snap up her story. She didn't notice the two locals who sat at the end of the bar, listening with quiet smiles on their faces.

"Could you tell me a little about your plans?" Sally asked.

"I plan to track down the Loch Ness Monster and probably capture it," the great man said.

Sally seemed doubtful. "But in the past year hundreds of people have tried to do that. Why are you so sure that you will succeed where they failed?"

The explorer raised his eyebrows. "They were amateurs. I am an expert. I am a member of the Royal Geographical Society. You don't become a member of the Royal Geographical Society unless you are a skilled and experienced scientist."

"How do you plan to find Nessie?" a man called out, to Sally's annoyance. This was *her* interview.

Wetherall smiled. "By using science. This creature has been seen on land. There are reports of it crossing the road and diving back into the water. There are too many trees and cliffs for the creature to do this in many places. There are only a certain number of places where the creature can enter and leave the loch. I shall look there. That is the scientific way to do it."

"But how will you find traces where no one else has?" Sally asked quickly.

The great man stroked his fine moustache calmly. "Because, young lady, I *know* what I'm looking for."

At the corner of the bar one local turned to the other. "And when you know what you want to find you very often find it."

They left the hotel and laughed all the way back to their boarding house. As they stepped through the front door they paused. In the hallway was a stand to hold umbrellas. It was made from the foot of a hippopotamus. Carefully the two men began to take out the umbrellas and place them on the floor . . .

The report in the *Daily Mail* caused a sensation all over the world. Within a week the great explorer had found footprints of the monster, just as he'd said he would.

> "... It is a four-fingered beast and it has feet or pads about 20cm across ... I am convinced it can breathe like a hippopotamus or a crocodile. The tracks I found were only a few hours old, clearly demonstrating that the animal is in the neighbourhood where I expected to find it."

Everyone at the *Daily Mail* was delighted with Wetherall's story. Everyone, that is, except their reporter at Loch Ness. As the great explorer sat in the bar he was surrounded by admirers who wanted to hear his story. Everyone was buying him drinks. Everyone except the two locals who smiled quietly at the corner of the bar.

Sally pushed through to the great man. "Ah, my girl!" he called. "Happy with your story?"

She shook her head slowly. The crowd in the bar grew quiet as the reporter said softly, "There's been a report from some experts on the copies that you made of the footprints."

Wetherall looked at her sharply. "Confirming my theory," he said confidently.

"Er . . . no."

The bar was as silent as the bottom of Loch Ness.

"The report says that all the footprints are the same," Sally said carefully.

"Of course they're the same!" Wetherall exploded. "They're from the same creature, you stupid girl."

She shook her head. "No. I mean exactly the same. It's the same footprint over and over again."

For a while the crowd around him was silent. Suddenly someone called out, "So the Loch Ness Monster has only one leg!"

A roar of laughter broke out as Wetherall turned scarlet. "There must be some mistake!"

"Have to call it the *hop* Ness Monster! Can you imagine a twenty-ton tennis ball? Boing! Boing! Boing!" another man cried.

Wetherall fled. In fact he resigned from the Royal Geographical Society not long after and went all the way back to Africa.

And in the bar room of the lakeside hotel two locals took out a parcel and unwrapped it on the bar. The hippopotamus foot stood there while the bar room crowd jeered, "Boing! Boing! Boing!"

It was the first of many such tricks played with the legend of the Loch Ness Monster.

After all, if you know what you want to find you very often find it . . .

Loch Ness Monster – FACT FILE

1.   If the creature in the loch is indeed a survivor from prehistoric times then there can be no Loch Ness *Monster*. If there *is* anything then there must be a family of Loch Ness *Monsters* for them to have bred and survived.

2.   There have been 10 000 *reported* sightings but only about 3 000 of these have been *recorded*. There are about 20 photographs of 'things' in Loch Ness and 25 films or videos. There seems to be a curse on attempts to photograph the monster. Many sightings have been disbelieved because cameras jammed at a vital moment or the film turned out mysteriously blank. Underwater radar explorations (sonar) have come up with some fakes, some mistakes (shoals of fish) and some blank results. Underwater photographs taken in 1975 have produced pictures that could be the flipper of a type of water dinosaur called a Plesiosaur. Plesiosaurs are thought to have become extinct millions of years ago.

3.   Loch Ness is the largest body of fresh water in the British Isles. It is over 300 metres deep in places and 22 miles (35 km) long. Its size makes it hard to explore and the colour of the water adds to the problems. Peat is washed down from the mountains around and makes the water dark brown. On the other hand Loch Ness would be a good place for a monster to live because it is full of fish: salmon, trout and eels. Some people believe

that the monsters escape underwater detection by hiding in deep caves. But there are no underwater caves in Loch Ness. This has been proved by underwater radar scans. There are, however, underwater currents which cause 'standing waves' to appear even on the calmest of days. These often have been mistaken for monstrous 'humps'.

4.   A clear and 'razor sharp' film of the creature was apparently taken in the 1930s by a banker called Currie. But he refused to show the film until "the public takes such matters seriously." It was never shown, and since his death it has not been found.

5.   A whisky company offered a reward of a million pounds to anyone who could capture the Loch Ness Monster. Their money is safe. For, if someone did present them with a real monster, it would be worth many, many millions of pounds in television, newspaper, film and book rights.

6.   Many of the witness reports are alike – and that suggests they have really seen something. They agree that the monster is 8 to 12 metres in length, with dark, thick skin and a small head on the end of a long neck. But not all witnesses are *reliable*. Mr and Mrs Spicer provided a sensational witness report of the monster crossing the road in front of their car on 22 July 1933. At first Mr Spicer said it was 2 metres long . . . but three years later he was saying it could have been 9 metres long.

7.   Some people don't believe Nessie is a creature at all, but a spaceship from Venus. Others are convinced it is the ghost of an ancient creature that haunts the loch. In 1973 The Reverend D. Omand tried to 'exorcise' the ghost with prayers.

8.   Scientists have tried to explain the monster in many ways. They say witnesses saw large otters, giant eels, seals, swimming deer, diving birds, rotting tree-trunks, shoals of fish and even whales.

9.   Old stories tell of an island in the loch which was swallowed up one night, and of a lazy monk from St Cummein. He refused to plough the land beside the church; a monstrous water-horse from the loch ploughed it for him, then vanished . . . taking the lazy monk with it! Ireland has many *loughs* (their name for lochs) and several tales of Saints defeating *lough piasts* (lake monsters): Saint Mochua of Balla thwarted a monster in a Connaught lough while Saint Patrick tricked a monster into imprisoning itself in a large barrel.

10.   A film company went to Loch Ness in 1969 to make a film in which Nessie had to appear. They hired a submarine to tow a model Nessie for the film. As the submarine explored the loch its sonar picked up the image of 'a large moving target' following! Was Nessie looking for a friend?

MONSTER A·P·E·S

Nine million years ago a breed of giant ape roamed the plains and forests of southern Asia. For eight-and-a-half million years they survived the hardships of weather and wild animals. Then, just half a million years ago there came another, smaller ape that drove them to extinction.

The old giant apes — scientists call them *Gigantopithecus* – had strength.

The new, smaller apes – scientists call them *Homo Erectus* – had brains. They made tools and weapons from stone, bone and wood. They made fire. They made *you*. They were the first humans.

Humans used their cunning and their weapons to take the best food and the best shelter from the giant apes. So the giant apes, old Gigantopithecus, died out. Or did they . . .?

The Yeti

Lhakpa Sherpani was cold. Even in the summer months it is cold in the Himalayan mountains of Nepal. But she huddled into her goatskin jacket and prodded the cattle with a pointed stick.

"Lhakpa! Take the cattle up the mountain," her mother had ordered. "But make sure they're back before nightfall! You don't want any accidents, do you?"

Lhakpa had pulled a face. "No, Mother." She was a big girl now – nineteen years old this summer. She didn't need to be told to be careful.

"And don't let the animals stray too near the ledges," the woman had gone on. "If one of them is killed we'll go hungry this winter!"

"No, mother," she sighed as she stretched sleepily before going to collect the four Tibetan cattle, the yak, from the pen.

Now the fat, slow yak lumbered up the path and swung their long-horned heads from side to side in time with their plodding pace.

After an hour's climb the girl stopped and let her cattle graze just below the snow-line of the mountain. She sat with her back to a rock. It sheltered her from the wind that always moaned through the mountains. The sun was warm on her tanned face. She ate a little of the cheese and bread her mother had packed, then leaned back and looked lazily down the valley.

The sun on the distant mountains dazzled her and she closed her brown eyes to rest. Slowly she slipped into a shallow sleep. She hardly knew she'd dozed off when she opened her eyes with a start. Something had wakened her. She didn't know what.

The wind had whipped a cloud around the mountain as she slept. The thin mist crawled down her neck.

But that wasn't what had awakened her. She jumped to her feet nervously. The yak! They were huddled together and moving up the mountain at a trot. It was as if they were running away from something.

Lhakpa called them but they swerved away with frightened bellows. Suddenly, from the corner of her eye she saw something moving behind a boulder. An arm. An arm waving to the yak and driving them towards the edge of a steep cliff where they would be cornered.

The girl gasped as the creature jumped out from behind the rock and raced after the terrified animals. Lhakpa had never seen such a creature before but she knew at once what it was. She'd heard the village stories since she was a tiny child.

"Yeti!" she cried.

But she hadn't time to think of what the monster might do to her. All she was thinking of was her mother's warning. If she lost an animal then the family would go hungry that winter.

The creature was well under two metres tall but twice as wide as the girl. It grabbed the first yak by the horns and twisted. The yak screamed and fell in a tangled heap. Its neck was broken.

"No-o-o!" Lhakpa screamed and the creature turned to face her. Its hair was thick and black below the waist, more a golden brown above it. The Yeti's fingers were thick, with nails like claws. The monster's face was almost human.

It ignored the girl and went after a second yak which it wrestled down with a single twist of its huge arms. At last Lhakpa reached the Yeti and thrashed wildly with her fists against the body – as solid as Everest itself.

The creature snorted and waved a hand at her as if swatting a fly. It caught the mountain girl on the jaw and sent her tumbling down the mountain slope.

This time it took her longer to awake. When she did her jaw felt broken and her sight was blurred. The sun was low in an amber sky and the freezing night was sliding over the mountains.

She stumbled back to the village with her tale of horror. At first all she could say through her swollen mouth was, "Yeti! Yeti!"

Her mother smoothed her hair gently and wiped her face with a damp cloth. Her father raged, "She fell asleep again! Tell the truth, girl, you fell asleep again! The yak went over the ledge! Isn't that right?"

"Yeti! Yeti!" she moaned.

No one wanted to search the mountain that night. But at first light the next day the villagers gathered sticks and knives and set off grimly up the path to the grazing grounds.

They found no Yeti. But they found five dead yak, and one had had its throat torn out by something with terrible claws. The rest had had their necks broken by something with terrible strength.

Lhakpa's father stared at the white wilderness above the snowline. At the rocks and ravines, the cliffs and the mist-shrouded snowfields that could hide an army of monsters. He nodded. "Sorry, Lhakpa," he muttered to himself. "You were right. Yeti."

Yeti – FACT FILE

1.   Yeti are often called 'Abominable Snowmen' because they live above the snow-line of the Himalayas, but most reports agree that they are brown in colour, not white like a snowman.

2.   'Yeti' is a Tibetan word meaning 'dweller among the high rocks.'

3.   A Chinese book written in the 1700s has drawings of Tibetan wildlife. It includes a picture of a heavy, hairy, human-like creature. The head comes to a furry point, the face is whitish with deep-sunken, red eyes and its arms dangle almost to its knees.

4.   There have been more sightings of Yeti footprints than of the creature itself. It has wide, five-toed feet which some say could be from a langur monkey. Others believe that the sightings have been of yellow snow-bears.

5.   The world's highest mountain is Mount Everest in the heart of Yeti country. The first man to climb that mountain was Sir Edmund Hillary in 1953. Seven years later he returned to the Himalayas at the head of an expedition to find the famous Yeti. He didn't find one. But Yeti scalps were said to be held by Tibetan monasteries. Sir Edmund brought one back. Scientists examined it. The 'scalp' turned out to be an old monk's hat made from goatskin!

6. No remains of anything like a complete Yeti have ever been found, though part of a mummified hand was found at Pangboche, Nepal, in the 1950s. It was described by some zoologists as 'almost human' and 'similar in some respects to that of Neanderthal man.'

7. There are no reports of Yeti carrying off humans – but there are reports of unexplained disappearances in the Sikkim region of the Himalayas where no traces have ever been found. A Norwegian uranium prospector, Jan Frostis, did claim that in 1948, he was attacked and his shoulder badly mauled by a Yeti he met near Zemu Gap in Sikkim.

8. A Tibetan story tells how a Yeti once slept on the roof of a yak-herder's hut at night to enjoy the warmth from the fire. The terrified herder put yak dung on the fire and smoked the Yeti away!

9. Sir Tashi, the religious leader of a Tibetan province, used to claim that the Yeti would come and see him on the 29th of each month. If the Yeti pushed Sir Tashi then the man would quietly say, "Come now, that's enough of that," and the creature would leave.

10. While the Tibetans have known about the Yeti for hundreds of years the first outsider to see footprint evidence was the British explorer, Major Waddell, in 1889. The first British resident in Nepal, B. H. Hodgson, described a creature he'd never seen before which "moved erectly, was covered in long, dark hair and had no tail."

Sasquatch

Monsters have feelings too. At least they do if we believe Albert Ostman's incredible story. Albert Ostman was a lumberjack working in British Columbia which later became known for its huge ape man called Bigfoot in the United States and Sasquatch over the border in Canada. Albert was camping out in the forest one night when he was suddenly picked up and carried off by a very strange creature. When this story happened in 1924 Mr Ostman didn't tell many about his amazing experience. Those he did tell thought that he was mad! He said no more about it for thirty-three years. Then, in 1957, stories were published about a monster ape in north-west America. It was given the name of a native American legend – Sasquatch.

This persuaded Ostman to break his silence. He took an oath before a Justice of the Peace that the story was true. People who heard Mr Ostman tell this story, believe it. He died some years later still swearing that this account is correct in every detail. Read his own words and make up your mind.

"I was inside my sleeping bag and being carried like a sack of potatoes. The only thing in sight was a huge hand clutching the neck of the bag. It was a rough journey, and it seemed to go on forever, but I guess it was about three hours. Finally he stopped and let me down. Then he dropped my packsack, I could hear the cans rattle. Then I heard some chatter – some kind of talk I didn't understand.

The ground was sloping so when he let go of my sleeping bag I rolled over head first downhill. I got my head out and got some air. I tried to straighten my legs and crawl out, but my legs were numb. It was still dark. I couldn't see what my captors looked like. I tried to massage my legs to get some life in them and get my shoes on.

53

I could hear now it was at least four of them. They were standing round me chattering non-stop. I knew then that I was with the Sasquatch.

As it grew lighter I could make them out. Four of them all right. Big and covered in short thick hair. Seemed to be two parents and two youngsters, a boy and a girl. The young fellow must have been eleven to eighteen years old but he was way over two metres tall. He had wide jaws, narrow forehead.

The old lady was even taller than the boy. She was not built for beauty or for speed. The man's eye teeth were longer than the rest of his teeth, but not long enough to be called tusks. The old man must have been two-and-a-half metres tall. Big barrel chest and a hump on his back. His finger-nails were like chisels. The soles of their feet seemed to be padded like a dog's foot and the big toe was longer than the rest and very strong.

They didn't seem to want to harm me so I decided to stay where I was till I could figure out a way to escape. I had some food, ammunition for the rifle, a knife, a few matches and some snuff. Didn't realize how useful that snuff was going to be.

They let me prepare my own food from the tins I had. But next day when I tried to leave the old man pushed me back. Seemed he and the girl were keeping a close watch on me. The old lady and the boy did the food collecting and housekeeping. They came home with arms full of grass and twigs as well as some kind of nuts that grow in the ground. The young fellow picked some kind of grass with long sweet roots. He gave me some one day. They tasted very sweet.

As the days went by I figured what they wanted me for. They wanted me for the young girl. Either as a pet . . . or as a mate! I knew then I had to escape. At the same time I didn't want to shoot my way out unless I had to.

The way I came to escape came through a lucky chance.

I discovered that the young fellow had a liking for my snuff. I waited for him and the old lady to go off on their errands into the forest. I thought I might be able to give the old man a taste of it while he was guarding me. Maybe throw it in his face or give him too much and choke him.

He watched me taking some. He came closer. I held the box towards him. Before I could throw it he snatched the whole box out of my hand. He swallowed it all in one. Not even a Sasquatch can take that!

After a few minutes his eyes began to roll over in his head and he was looking straight up. I could see he was sick. Then he grabbed my coffee can that was quite cold by this time. He emptied it into his mouth, grounds and all. That did no good.

He stuck his head between his legs and rolled forward a few times away from me. Then he began to squeal like a stuck pig. I grabbed my rifle. I said to myself, "This is it. If he comes for me I'll shoot him plumb between the eyes."

But he started for the spring. He wanted water. I packed my sleeping bag in my packsack with the few cans I had left.

That was when the young fellow came back and spotted me. He ran over to his mother. Then she began to squeal. I started for the opening in the wall – and I just made it. The old lady was right behind me. I fired one shot at the rock above her head. That frightened her enough to let me escape.

I must have run three miles in record time till I came to a logging camp and civilization once again."

Sasquatch – FACT FILE

1. Sasquatch does not like dogs. There are many reports of dogs being given a serious beating by the ape man.

2. Sasquatch does not appear to like baths either. His smell has been described as "like a skunk" or "like rotting flesh".

3. Sightings of Sasquatch have been linked with sightings of UFOs (Unidentified Flying Objects) and one idea is that Sasquatch is an alien. The first sighting of a footprint by a European was in 1811 when the explorer and trader, David Thompson, came across a whole trail of gigantic prints. He measured them at 35 cm long by 20 cm wide.

4. Most early sightings of Sasquatch were in the north-west United States. In some parts of the United States a similar monster is known as Bigfoot. In this part of the world there are thousands of square kilometres of mountain forests and few roads or towns, the ideal spot for a giant ape to live without being seen for years.

5. Some people believe that Sasquatch could be related to Yeti. They think Yeti could have crossed from Asia to America thousands of years ago when the two continents were joined by a land-bridge. However, they do not explain how the huge Yowie has been seen so much – for the Yowie lives in Australia!

6. In 1884 a young Sasquatch was seen from a train travelling through British Columbia (west Canada). The crew stopped the train and captured it. They named it Jacko and after going on show in the county it was sold to a circus. Jacko was a pretty small Sasquatch. Some experts believe he could have been a runaway chimpanzee.

7. In 1967 two men succeeded in capturing Bigfoot on about 6 metres of movie film. The film shows what could be a man in a gorilla skin – or what could be a real monster. If it is a fake then it's a very good one – people are still arguing about it. One scientist who has studied the film in minute detail still won't say it's a fake or a genuine film. All he will say is, "I couldn't see the zipper, and I still can't."

8. Sasquatch has been given the blame for some pretty nasty crimes. In 1910 the McLeod brothers went mining in the Nahanni Valley in the North West Territories of Canada. They were found with their heads cut off. Sasquatch was reported to have been seen in the area and was given the blame. The place became known as Headless Valley.

9. Bigfoot means big business in the United States. You can go on Bigfoot expeditions, stay in the Bigfoot Motel and eat Bigfoot burgers. But you can't shoot Bigfoot – at least not in California where it is a protected species.

10.   If a Sasquatch comes to your door, beware! It has been said it has the power to hypnotize you, or to trick you with its voice (like a ventriloquist). You should be able to recognize one because witnesses say their eyes glow red . . . or orange . . . or green – depending on which you choose to believe!

The Yowie of Australia

The Aborigines knew all about the hairy giant long before Europeans came to Australia. They had many names for the creature, but now it is generally called the Yowie. Australia has thousands of acres of bushland rarely visited by humans. It would be easy for a family of creatures to stay undiscovered for years.

But, as the settlers spread across the continent, sightings of an ape man began to be recorded. One, seen by Johnnie McWilliams in 1894, seemed a little less tough than the average monster.

Johnnie was on his way from his home in Snowball to the Jinden Post Office in New South Wales, when he saw "a big man covered with long hair." The Yowie was as shocked as Johnnie by the meeting and ran off across open country before disappearing over a hill. But the creature made a mistake – it kept its eyes on the boy as it ran, and didn't look where it was going. As a result it caught its foot against a log and gave a bellow of pain.

One of the clearest sightings was in 1912, also in New South Wales. Charles Harper was a Sydney surveyor who was camping with friends in the Currickbilly Mountains. Hearing a noise in the dark they threw some kindling on the fire and it flared up to give them a better look at the intruder. Charles Harper described it as . . .

"A huge man-like animal. It stood erect, not twenty metres from the fire, growling, grimacing, and thumping his breast with his huge hand-like paws. I looked round and saw one of my companions had fainted. He remained unconscious for some hours. The creature stood in one position for some time, sufficiently long to enable me to photograph him on my brain.

I should say its height when standing erect would be 5ft 8in to 5ft 10in [1.73 to 1.78 metres]. Its body, legs and arms were covered with long, brownish-red hair, which shook with every quivering movement of its body. The hair on its shoulder and back parts appeared in the subdued light of the fire to be jet black and long; but what struck me as extraordinary was the apparently human shape, but still so very different.

I will commence its detailed description with the feet, which only occasionally I could get a glimpse of. I saw that the metatarsal [foot] bones were very short, much shorter than in a human, but the toes were extremely long, indicating great grasping power in the feet. The shin-bone of the leg was much shorter than in a human. The thigh-bone was very long, out of proportion to the rest of the leg. The body frame was enormous, indicating immense strength and power of endurance. The arms and forepaws were extremely long and large, and very muscular, being covered with shorter hair. The head and face were very small, but very human. The eyes were large, dark and piercing, deeply set. A most horrible mouth was ornamented with two large and long canine teeth. When the jaws were closed they protruded over the lower lip. The stomach seemed like a sack hanging halfway down to the thighs. All this observation occupied a few minutes while the creature stood erect as if the firelight had paralysed him.

After a few more growls and thumping his breast he made off, the first few yards erect, then at a faster gait on all fours through the low scrub. Nothing would induce my companions to continue the trip, at which I was rather pleased, and returned as quickly as possible out of reach of the Australian gorillas, rare as they are."

The Yowie – FACT FILE

1.   Australian Yowie researcher, Rex Gilroy, has collected over 3000 reports of Yowie sightings.

2.   The Yowie has a lot in common with its Yeti and Bigfoot Sasquatch cousins: not only its size and its hairiness but its sickening smell too. One witness described it as being "like a public lavatory."

3.   A Yowie was shot in the Brindabella Mountains in New South Wales, but not killed. The Webb brothers, Joseph and William, saw one approach their camp at the turn of this century. When it refused to stop they took aim and fired, but the bullet failed to have any effect other than scaring the Yowie away. Reports of encounters with Sasquatch have suggested that it too is unhurt by bullets.

4.   Yowies are curious. They are reported watching humans at work, not interfering, but not afraid.

5.   Yowies, like Yeti, have been known to attack humans. In 1968 in a saw-milling settlement of Kookaburra, New South Wales, George Grey woke to find a greasy, hairy ape man on top of him. This one was only about 1.20 metres tall, so he was able to throw it off after a struggle, and run away.

6.   Like Sasquatch the reported sightings of Yowies increased in the 1970s.

7. A footprint left by a Yowie in 1912 showed only four toes.

8. One bold Yowie is said to have put its head around a door in Springbrook on the Gold Coast and stayed until someone threw a chair at it.

9. Some scientists argue against the possibility of Yowies existing, saying it doesn't make sense. The Yowie's description would make it a Primate (highest form of mammal, e.g. man, ape) – but the first and only Primates in Australia are human beings, and they arrived in boats. Every native Australian mammal is a marsupial (mammals with pouches, e.g. kangaroo).

10. Yowies make a sound like a pig's grunt. When upset they can roar like a bull.

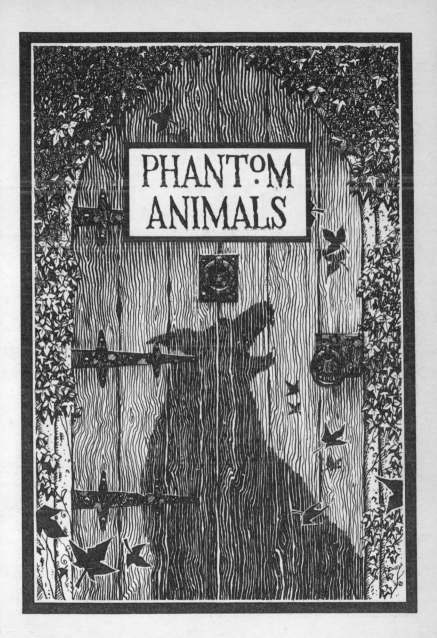

PHANTOM ANIMALS

"The moon was shining bright upon the clearing, and there in the centre lay the unhappy maid where she had fallen, dead of fear and fatigue. But it was not the sight of her body, nor was it that of Hugo Baskerville lying near her, which raised the hair upon the heads of those three men. But it was that, standing over Hugo, and plucking at his throat, there stood a foul thing, a great black beast, shaped like a hound, yet larger than any hound that ever mortal eye has rested upon. And even as they looked the thing tore the throat out of Hugo Baskerville. As it turned its blazing eyes and dripping jaws upon them, the three shrieked with fear and rode for dear life, still screaming across the moor. One, it is said, died that very night of what he had seen, and the other two were broken men for the rest of their days."

The Hound of The Baskervilles by Sir Arthur Conan Doyle

Of course the great Sherlock Holmes didn't believe in monstrous Black Dogs. After a couple of murders he discovers that the hound is just a big vicious dog, half starved so it will kill, and painted in luminous liquid to glow in the dark and scare its victims into the nasty bog known as Grimpen Mire.

It's a great story. Not a word of it is true. But Conan Doyle didn't make up all the elements of the story. For the legend of a great hound has been passed down for hundreds of years. Some stories are in the imagination of frightened people – people walking along country roads at night before street lighting was thought of. Strange scufflings in the hedgerows, the snort of a curious cow as it poked its head over a wall. The barking foxes in the forest, the screech of a creature caught by an owl. Enough to make anyone imagine they were being chased by a nightmare hound.

But some stories are not so easily explained. Some even have evidence. If you want to find the great Black Dog then England is probably the best place, though they have been reported all over the world, and, while most English counties have their stories, the county of Suffolk seems to be the home of the beast.

And in Suffolk the most likely place would be the peaceful village of Blythburgh . . .

The Black Dog of Blythburgh

The land around Blythburgh is flat. Some time in the distant past it struggled up out of the sea. But now the sea is slowly taking it back.

Just down the coast the waves are eating into the soft cliffs. One by one the villages have slid into those waves. They say that on a stormy night you can hear the church bells chiming from one sea-swallowed village. Dunwich it was called. A ghost village now.

A couple of miles inland, over rugged heath and forest, stands a church. Taller and grander than most country churches, it looks out over the deep, dark marshes. It is Blythburgh Church, known as the Cathedral of the Marshes.

Even today it is peaceful in summer, lonely when the cold winds whip off the North Sea . . . and menacing when it begins to grow dark. When eerie sounds echo over the marshes; when old tales of monster dogs become believable. When you can understand the terror that gripped the folk of Blythburgh four hundred years ago.

Sunday 4 August 1577

It began in Bungay village church just seven miles away. The Suffolk sky is vast at any time – no hills to shorten the horizon. That day it towered over the countryside with great grey menacing clouds. The distant rumbles warned the people of a storm to come. They hurried for the shelter of the church, little knowing that there was no safety there. The storm hurried nearer. Then it broke above the churches: the one in Bungay and the one in Blythburgh. Abraham Fleming was in Bungay church that day and told what happened next . . .

"Immediately hereupon there appeared to the congregation a horrible likeness of a dog, black in colour. At the sight of the dog, and of the fearful flashes that were there seen, many of the people believed that Doomsday was already come.

This black dog (or the devil in the likeness of a dog) ran along down the body of the church with great swiftness and incredible haste. It ran among the people in a visible form and shape and passed between two persons as they were kneeling upon their knees, seemingly in prayer. It wrung the necks of them both at one instant. Clean backwards, so far that in a moment, as they kneeled, they strangely died.

There was at the same time another wonder wrought. For the same dog, remaining in the same shape and form, passed by another man in the congregation. He gave him such a bite on the back that the man was soon drawn together and shrunk up, like a piece of leather scorched in a hot fire; or like the mouth of a purse drawn together with a string.

That man, although he was so strangely attacked, died not, but is thought as yet alive. That is marvellous in the eyes of men and an amazing thing to the mind."

But the Black Dog hadn't finished yet. He hurried to the church at Blythburgh, seven miles away, and caused similar chaos . . .

"Placing himself upon the main roof beam suddenly he swung down through the church. There, as before, he slew two men and a lad. He burned the hand of another person that was there among the rest of the company of whom several were blasted."

Abraham Fleming was the pastor of a London church. An honest man?

In Bungay market place today they have a weather vane, but instead of the usual cockerel they have the image of a leaping Black Dog.

And what has Blythburgh Church to show? Look closely at the main front door. There you'll see some black scorch marks. They say the Black Dog left them as he raced into the church.

Monster Black Dogs – FACT FILE

1.   Black Dog monsters have been reported all over Europe, North and South America but their origins seem to be the British Isles. One is reported as early as 1127 in the *Anglo-Saxon Chronicle*. A pack of Black Dogs kept the monks of Peterborough awake from Lent until Easter as they hunted the fens of East Anglia. They were led by a huntsman dressed in jet black.

2.   You can tell a monster Black Dog from a normal dog by its size and its eyes. They are often very large – "as tall as a mantelpiece" – and have eyes, large as saucers, that glow. In fact the Black Dog of Winsford Hill in Somerset is said to fade slowly until only the glowing eyes are left. The Kludde of Belgium is easier to spot because it is a huge Black Dog with wings that walks on its hind legs; it also makes the sound of a clanking chain. It uses the chain to beat its victims. It is no use trying to outrun the Kludde. The faster you run the faster it follows, slithering between trees like a giant snake.

3.   Black Dog monsters don't often make much noise. Their footsteps are silent and they rarely bark. But when they do make a noise it is odd: footsteps like the clopping of a horse, a blood-chilling howl or even a devilish laugh. Be particularly careful of the ones that talk. A man met one on the road to Woolpit in Suffolk which said to him, "I shall want you within the week!"

. . . and he died the next night. A similar dog was said to roam the graveyards of Chicago in the 1940s. But it was white. To see the White Dog meant certain death within the year.

4. In the north of England the Black Dog is known as Trash, Skryker or the Barguest. In East Anglia it is Shuck, Scarfe or Skeff. Hooter is its name in Midland England and Hairy Jack in Lincolnshire. The Irish call their Black Dog, Pooka.

5. If you try to pat a monster Black Dog you may find that your hand goes right through it. However some people report that the dog vanishes if you try to stroke it. However, a man tried to stroke a Black Dog which blocked his road at Hatfield Peverell, Essex, in 1850. He clearly believed that it was a normal dog. He was burnt to ashes along with his horse and cart.

6. The Black Dog sometimes appears with an unusual head: the head of a monk (Clopton Hall near Great Bealings, Suffolk), the head of an ape (Balsham and West Wratting in Suffolk), or sometimes with no head at all.

7. Black Dogs don't seem to have a lot of road sense. There are several reports of motorists running "into" Black Dogs as they dash across the road. However, when the motorist gets out to see if the animal is hurt, it has vanished.

8. Real pet dogs and police dogs are reported to be terrified in the presence of the monster Black Dogs. Two police dogs got into a fight with an invisible Black Dog in France in 1939. The battle lasted two minutes and ended with the death of one of the police dogs.

9. Black Dogs are often seen near water (as with the case in Blythburgh Marshes), near churches and near crossroads.

10. In the 1950s a Black Dog terrorized the area of Kettleness near Whitby. Strangely in Bram Stoker's story, *Dracula*, the writer described the vampire coming ashore at Kettleness . . . in the form of a huge hound!

Some monster animals, like the Black Dogs, are clearly known animals. But known animals become mysterious when they appear – and disappear – in the wrong places at the wrong times. They can behave with great ferocity and terrorize a community. One such animal is the kangaroo. Common enough in the outback of Australia – monstrous in the towns and cities of twentieth-century America . . .

The Phantom Kangaroo

"Granny, can I go out to play?" the girl asked.

The woman looked up sharply from her sewing. Then she glanced at the window. "It's getting a little dark, Lucy. Best not go outside now."

The woman poked the fire until the log crackled and flared, then returned to her sewing.

Pouting Lucy flung herself into an armchair. "Mom lets me go out at this time. It's only six o'clock."

"Your mom's left me in charge. She'd never forgive me if something happened to you," Granny explained.

The girl wriggled and scowled. "Why can't I go out, Granny?"

The woman put down her sewing and leaned forward in her chair. "Lucy, it isn't safe to go out on the streets after dark."

"Why?"

Granny sighed and looked over the top of her spectacles at the girl. "Someone or something might get you."

"What thing, Granny?" Lucy asked with a nervous laugh.

The woman's eyes shifted to the flickering shadows in the corner of the room and she whispered, "The kangaroo!"

Now Lucy's laugh was scornful. "Kangaroo! Kangaroo! Oh, come on, you're not trying to tell me there's a nasty kangaroo out there waiting to get me? Even Mom never tries that sort of story on me."

But Granny didn't laugh. "Your mom wasn't born when the great kangaroo scare hit America. But I was. I was just about your age."

"Kangaroo scare? People were scared of a kangaroo! Were you scared of it?" Lucy giggled.

Granny looked into the amber flames and shook her head. "Older and wiser people than I were scared of the phantom kangaroo. Priests and policemen and tough old truck drivers were scared of him. I was just plain terrified."

Lucy shuffled foward onto the edge of her seat. "Tell me about it, Gran."

"It started in South Pittsburg, Tennessee, not far from where I was brought up. My pa came in all excited one night and read the newspaper report to us kids. It was some time in January 1934. The Reverend W. J. Handcock saw the beast in a field and described it to the newspaper. I remember Pa reading that report clear as yesterday. 'It was fast as lightning and looked like a giant kangaroo running and leaping across the field.' Then it went on to tell of a large dog being killed . . ."

"Could have been run down by a truck," Lucy objected.

Granny shook her head. "The dog was killed . . . and eaten. So were lots of chickens in the nearby farms!"

"Did they catch it?" Lucy asked eagerly.

"The police took the Reverend seriously – him being a minister and all – and they had a big search for the beast. They never found a thing."

"You reckon the priest was lying?" Lucy asked, a little shocked.

Granny shrugged. "If he was, then so were lots of others. Someone came up with the story that they'd seen the kangaroo escaping from a farm with a dead sheep tucked underneath each arm."

Lucy shuddered. "And they never saw it again?"

"Not for fifteen years. I remember I'd just finished college that year when that old kangaroo turned up again. This time it was up at Grove City, Ohio. A driver saw something hop across the beams of his headlights as he drove along at night."

Lucy squinted at her grandmother. "Are you sure you're telling me the truth?"

The woman rose stiffly from her chair and went to the old dresser by the kitchen door. She sifted through some old papers until she came to a scrap-book filled with faded photos and newspaper cuttings. She sat on the arm of Lucy's chair and pointed out the pages. "I was interested in the story, seeing the first had happened so near where I was a girl. I kept some of the cuttings. Here we are. The driver was Louis Staub . . ."

Lucy read on, " 'It was about five-and-a-half feet [1.68 metres] high, hairy and brownish. It had a pointed head. It looked like a kangaroo but it appeared to jump on all fours. I'm certain it wasn't a deer.' " The girl looked up. "Maybe it *was* a kangaroo! Maybe it escaped from the local zoo!"

"They thought of that. None were ever reported missing. Same as when children kept reporting a 'big bunny' they saw in Coon Rapids, Minnesota."

The girl frowned at the fire. "That was still way before I was born. If I go out to play there sure won't be any kangaroo waiting to tuck me under his hairy old arm."

Her grandmother said nothing. She simply turned the page to some more newspaper cuttings. These were not so yellowed with age.

" 'Eighteenth of October, 1974,' " Lucy read. " 'Chicago!' "

"That's right. A man called the police and said there was a kangaroo hopping around his front porch. The police didn't believe it of course, but they had to send a couple of patrol men out to investigate. And what do you think they found when they got there?"

Lucy's eyes were wide and her mouth slightly open. "What?"

"A kangaroo, of course!"

"Did they shoot it?" the girl gasped.

"No. They didn't have the heart. They chased it into a back alley and tried to catch it. But it started lashing out, the way they do, with those big back legs, and the police backed off. In the end it hopped over a fence and escaped. They had lots of reports from people claiming they'd seen a kangaroo rummaging through their garbage bins. One newspaper boy even claimed it hopped up to him and stared. The newspapers had a great time of it."

The woman pointed to a headline and Lucy giggled as she read it out loud. " 'KANGAROO STAYS A JUMP AHEAD OF THE POLICE.' "

"There were more reports from towns to the west of Chicago – here's one from Plano, Illinois. Three young men driving along and one says, 'We almost ran over it. It jumped onto the road about twenty feet [6.1 metres] ahead of us . . . it landed on the road near the junction with the main road and there was no traffic. It sat up on its haunches and then jumped over a fence about five feet high [1.52 metres] and disappeared into the woods.' "

Lucy turned the page. "A few smaller reports from 1976 . . . Wisconsin . . . Colorado . . . Ohio. Wow! It sure gets around."

Her granny smiled and closed the book. "It could be anywhere, any time. It could be out there right now, waiting for some little girl to poke her nose out of the door. Then he'll just tuck her under his arm and hop off into the night."

The girl shivered and wriggled closer to the fire. She glanced towards the windows that showed the purple velvet sky closing in. Her grandmother closed the curtains and threw another log on the fire.

"It's getting a little cold out there," Lucy said softly. "Perhaps I'll just stay in and read a book."

Granny smiled and went back to her sewing.

Monster Phantom Animals – FACT FILE

1. Mysterious cats are almost as common as dogs. They are reported all over the world. They are blamed for savaging farm animals but are rarely caught or photographed. Zoos never admit to losing animals at the time of their appearance.

2. There are no reports of phantom kangaroos in Australia. However they do have the famous Bunyip that inhabits lakes or swamps and drags its victims down to their deaths. There are countless Bunyip stories – some refer to known animals, some to mythical beasts, but many to an unidentified monster. Twentieth-century reports are rare so it may now be extinct. It may have been a fresh-water seal . . . but they have only been known in Canada and parts of Asia. Aborigines thought of the Bunyip as a *demon* or a *spirit* and this is the most likely truth. The Bunyip is just a monster of legend.

3. A curious mongoose attracted a lot of publicity on the Isle of Man in 1931. It lived with the Irving family and thirteen-year-old Voirrey Irving taught it to talk. It declared its name was Gef. Several investigators heard it chatting away behind the panelled walls of the Irvings' farmhouse – but no one, except Voirrey, ever saw it. Was Gef a phantom mongoose . . . or the creation of a lonely teenage girl with a talent for ventriloquism?

4. A mysterious animal left a hundred miles of footprints in the snow. It happened in Devon in February 1855. The prints in the shape of a horse's hoof ran over roofs, crossed a river, appeared to enter and exit a drain-pipe and to leap over a 4-metre wall. In many places they stopped suddenly as if the creature had risen into the air. The explanations over the years have included badgers, cats, foxes, otters, cranes, donkeys, a pony with a broken shoe, rats, rabbits, squirrels and even toads. Of course an escaped kangaroo has been suggested. The most popular explanation at the time was that it was the Devil himself who had walked through Devon that night.

5. The Griffin was generally accepted as a purely imaginary beast: the body of a lion with the head and wings of an eagle. But in 1984 there were several sightings of such a creature in Brentford in London. It was said to be the size of a large dog and flew with a very slow flapping of its wings. Curiously the coat of arms of Brentford District Council shows two griffins supporting a shield . . . and Brentford Football club play at Griffin Park.

6. A vicious phantom monkey was commonly seen on a bridge over the Birmingham and Liverpool canal in the late 1870s. It scared horses and riders, but attempts to whip it failed when the whip passed straight through it. After one attack on 21 January 1879 the policeman investigating shrugged off the complaint with the

comment, "Oh, is that all, sir? I know what that was. That was the man-monkey, sir, as does come again at that bridge ever since the man was drowned in the canal."

SEA MONSTERS

Monsters seem to have lurked in the seas since the dawn of time. Sailors forced to stay at home on winter nights must have made up tales to thrill the children.

Fishermen today still tell tales of monstrous fish that they once caught . . . but in the struggle 'got away'. And every time the tale is told the fish grows slightly bigger. Was that how the legends of Ancient Greece began, with sailors returning and exaggerating their encounters with large fish or sea mammals?

But stories of *true* sea-monsters are hard to find before 1550 . . . and even then they are suspiciously unreal.

Olaus Magnus described one in the year of 1555. The monster had a large square head, with two great horns, and huge eyes. The creature could be seen at night because it glowed a firey red.

Again in 1555 a giant squid was washed ashore along the Iceland coast. The tentacles were missing, but still it measured 18 metres. With its tentacles it would have measured a monstrous 30 metres, maybe more. These are often said to be the first reports of some true ocean giants.

But a well-recorded, and most reliable, early report comes from the ambassador to Venice, no less. After a visit to England back in 1532 he sent this report back to his senate . . .

"In the month of August this sea of ours stranded near Tynemouth a dead animal of exceeding great size, which for the most part has been already pulled apart; and what remains is of such bulk that 100 wains [wagons] could scarcely carry it away.

Those who first saw this animal, and described it as precisely as they could, say it measured 30 yards or 90 feet [28 metres]; from the belly to the fin on the back, which was buried in the sand, the length was eight or nine yards [8 metres].

The exact dimensions cannot be ascertained because, when I went to see this animal on 27 August, it emitted such a stench as to be almost unbearable; but its back, covered by the sand, is some three yards broad [2.7 metres] so that the sea beats upon it daily and the waves break over it. The opening of the mouth is $6\frac{1}{2}$ yards [6 metres]; the length of each jaw $7\frac{1}{2}$ yards [7 metres]. Altogether it is as big as a large oak.

It has thirty ribs on its sides, and for the most part they are 21 feet long [6.5 metres] and one half foot [15 centimetres] in diameter.

It has three bellies like very large caves, and thirty throats, five of which are larger than the rest; it has two wings or fins for swimming, each of which is 15 feet long [4.5 metres] so that ten oxen could scarcely draw one of them away. Adhering to the palate were certain horny *laminae* [thin, bony plates] having on one side in number upwards of 1000, one of which I send thee. It is not a lie, Polydore, but a thing perfectly true, though they are not all of one size.

The length from the beginning of the head to the aperture of the mouth is 7 yards [6.5 metres]. Concerning the tongue some persons differ; the majority say that it was 7 yards long [6.5 metres].

A certain man having entered the body to pull it to pieces, fell, and would have been drowned had he not clung to a rib.

The space between the eyes is 6 yards [5.5 metres] and the nostrils are very disproportioned to so huge a frame for they resemble those of an ox. The tail is forked and notched like a saw.

In its head were two large holes from which it is supposed to spout forth water as if by tubes. It had no teeth, so people guess that it is not a whale, as whales have very large teeth; but in its mouth were the horny *laminae* mentioned above."

A true monster – even the largest fish today (a whale shark) is only half that length. If it wasn't an unknown monster then it could only have been a blue whale – the largest and heaviest creature of all time. The largest weigh as much as 3135 average men – that's more than enough to fill those thirty wagons! Blue whales have been hunted almost to extinction by man. But, back in 1532, they could just have grown that big.

The more men sailed the seas, the stranger were the things they saw. And the stranger their tales became of giant squids that sank their ships, and mermaids combing out their hair.

Mr Cobbin of Durban saw a beast from the boat *Silvery Wave* . . . he *said*. It had a head like a bull, a back covered in rainbow-coloured scales like armour and it raced through the water with a caterpillar wiggle. He claimed it was over 1000 yards (925 metres) long!

If we believe him then this beast was *ten times* larger than the blue whale and about three times as long as the Eiffel Tower is high. There have even been reports of a sea monster thirty metres long, the shape of a tadpole and striped black and yellow.

But some stories are more believable than others and need to be looked at more carefully. Stories like the case of Morgawr . . .

The Morgawr

The old Cornish man sat by the tavern fire and stared at the dancing flames. "Of course there's a monster out there in the bay," he chuckled. "Haven't you read the papers?"

The young man grinned. "I am the papers – at least I'm a reporter. Dave's the name. That's what I'm doing in Falmouth. I've come to follow up the stories about this funny fish."

The old man looked at him sharply and pointed his pipe stem at the reporter. "Don't go calling her no 'funny fish'. Her name's Morgawr."

"How do you spell that?" the young man asked.

"I didn't stop to ask her," the old man replied sourly.

"You've seen it too then?" the other asked eagerly. "I'm just off to meet a man who says he can conjure up this Morgawr with magic."

"That'll be the feller they call 'Doc' – not a proper doctor, of course. More like a witch-doctor."

"You don't believe it then?" Dave asked.

The man sucked on his pipe stem and shrugged. "Certainly lots of strange things seem to happen when he's around. You have to give him that. And not just Morgawr swimming around in Falmouth Bay."

"But you said you'd seen Morgawr yourself," Dave urged.

"Ahh! That was fifty years ago, back in 1926. We were out trawling when we caught her in the nets – twenty-foot (6.1 metres) long with an eight-foot (2.4 metres) tail. But it tore its way out of our nets with its huge beak!"

"A beak?" Dave laughed. He wasn't sure if the fisherman was making fun of him. But the old man looked serious enough. He fished inside his wallet for an old piece of newspaper. "Here's the report from the time – and one from 1876."

The young reporter peered at them carefully. The 1876 report was yellowed and wrinkled but Dave managed to read it.

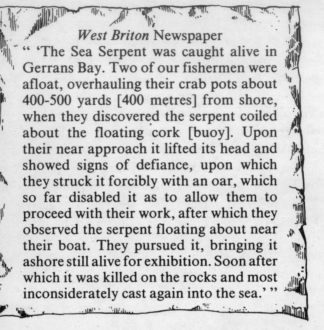

West Briton Newspaper

" 'The Sea Serpent was caught alive in Gerrans Bay. Two of our fishermen were afloat, overhauling their crab pots about 400-500 yards [400 metres] from shore, when they discovered the serpent coiled about the floating cork [buoy]. Upon their near approach it lifted its head and showed signs of defiance, upon which they struck it forcibly with an oar, which so far disabled it as to allow them to proceed with their work, after which they observed the serpent floating about near their boat. They pursued it, bringing it ashore still alive for exhibition. Soon after which it was killed on the rocks and most inconsiderately cast again into the sea.' "

"But the monster was dead!" Dave objected.

The old man's watery blue eyes twinkled. "Maybe it had relatives. Fifty years later I saw it."

Dave nodded. "Fifty years, eh? And fifty years after that it pops up again."

"That's right," the fisherman agreed.

The reporter flipped through his notebook. "September 1975 – last year in fact – Mrs Scott of Falmouth saw a long-necked, hump-backed monster off Pendennis Point. It had horns and bristles on its neck. Let me see . . . reports over the winter . . . and then on 5 March the local paper and some photos from a woman calling herself Mary F."

"That's right. Looks like an elephant waving its trunk, except the trunk is its neck."

Dave shook his head. "But Mary F. never came forward and she said the negatives were sold to an American. Bit suspicious that. She doesn't name this mysterious American – almost as if she didn't want the negatives examined."

The fisherman lit his pipe with a spill from the fire. "Lots of other reports this summer, though. Respectable people, too! Dentists, bankers from London, company directors."

"And witches," Dave grinned. "There's a report here of three girls coming down and swimming naked in the bay chanting magic spells!"

The old man chuckled. "Didn't put old Morgawr off though! She still kept appearing. That's when that Doc feller came down to investigate."

Dave glanced at his watch. "That reminds me. I'm meeting him on the Helford River bank in five minutes. Says he may be able to conjure up that fishy fraud for me!"

"Not a fish – a monster!" the old man reminded him.

Dave laughed as he stepped out into the raw November afternoon. "I'll believe it when I see it."

But Dave wasn't laughing when he returned to the inn that evening. The old fisherman was back at his fireside seat with a mug of ale and that smouldering pipe. Dave sat down heavily.

"Well? Did Doc introduce you to Morgawr?" the man asked.

The reporter shook his head, uncertain. "I'm not sure. I'll know when the film in my camera is developed."

"Morgawr let you take her picture then?"

And Dave told his story. He'd met the magician and begun to interview him. Then he'd taken some pictures of Doc waving a wand over the waves. All good entertaining stuff for the paper. "Doc wanted to take a few pictures of his own," Dave explained. "While I was waiting for him I kept warm by throwing some stones for my dog to chase. That's when Doc cried out that there was something out in the river – a dark head rising out of the water. I grabbed my camera and tried to fit a telephoto lens. But it was cold and I was fumbling with excitement."

"Morgawr has that effect on people," the old man nodded.

"But I made it in the end. I thought it was a seal's head, but then it raised itself up out of the water and the neck was too long and narrow for a seal."

"Sounds like the Morgawr I saw," the fisherman agreed. "What happened then?"

Dave looked sheepishly into his beer. "Then the dog started barking in the excitement – and Morgawr dived."

"So now you believe in the Sea Giant?"

"The what?"

"That's what Morgawr means in the old Cornish language – Sea Giant."

The young reporter stirred the fire with a stick and sighed. "I'll wait till I see the photos."

But Dave was disappointed. Just as with the Loch Ness Monster the camera was mysteriously faulty. The winder didn't work so the three photos came out on one jumbled frame. Doc's photos were taken without a telephoto lens and were too small to prove anything.

Dave was never sure what he'd seen.

The magician and monster-investigator, Doc Shiels, went on to take photos of the Loch Ness Monster the next year. So he's quite sure that unknown creatures of the sea still exist.

Many other people claim to have seen the Sea Giant and are ready to swear that monsters do exist in the sea.

And, of course, the old Cornish fishermen always believed in their Morgawr.

Sea Monsters – FACT FILE

1. In 1965 Dr Bernard Heuvelmans, a zoologist, looked at nearly 600 reported sightings of sea monsters. He decided there were nine types of sea monster:

Saurian – crocodile types;

Super Eel – snake-like but probably a fish;

Super Otter – a long-tailed mammal;

Many-finned – long, jointed mammal with triangular fins;

Many-humped – long mammal, blunt head, short neck, pair of flippers, humps along back;

Long-necked – a tailless seal type;

Seahorse – like the Long-necked but with large eyes, whiskers and a mane;

Giant Tadpole – yellow, tadpole-shaped, rarest sighting;

Giant Turtle – like the Archelon of the Mesozoic Era.

He decided that 358 sightings could not be explained as hoaxes, mistakes or confusion with known creatures and were therefore true.

2. One of the longest-lasting sea-monster legends concerns mermaids and mermen. A fish-tailed god is mentioned in the Bible. More recently South Africa's *Pretoria News* reported a mermaid sighting in a Lusaka storm-drain on 20 December 1977. The creature was "European woman from the waist up, whilst the rest of

her body was shaped like the back end of a fish, and covered with scales." Mermaid sightings are often explained as mistaken sea-mammals such as manatees and dugongs. But others believe that millions of years ago our human ancestors emerged from the seas to live on the land – merfolk are the ancestors who chose to stay in the sea.

3.   In 1913 there was a report of a young sea monster off the coast of Australia. Oscar Davies, a Tasmanian State mining prospector, and his mate, W. Harris, saw it on the beach at sunset.

"It was fifteen feet [4.5m] long. It had a small head, a thick arched neck passing gradually into the barrel of the body. It had no definite tail and no fins. It was furred, the coat in appearance resembling that of a horse of a chestnut colour, well groomed and shining. It had four distinct legs and left distinct footprints. These showed circular impressions with a diameter (measured) of nine inches [22.8 cm] and the marks of claws about seven inches [17.8 cm] long extending outwards from the body. The creature travelled very fast. A kangaroo dog followed it to the water. When disturbed it reared up and turned on its hind legs. Its height, standing on the four legs, would be from 3ft 6in to 4ft [1.07 to 1.22 metres]."

The men were familiar with the seals and sea-leopards of that coast but this monster was not one of them.

4.   There is more sea than land – it covers three-fifths of the Earth's surface. In places it is 6 miles (9.5 km) deep, and only a minute fraction has been explored. Enough room to give a home to many creatures that humans have never encountered.

5.   The largest whales are 30 metres long, the largest known fish (the whale shark) up to 18 metres long.

6.   Just when we think we know all the life forms in the oceans a new one is discovered – in 1937 a previously unknown beaked whale was washed ashore in New Zealand . . .

7.   . . . and, just when we think all the prehistoric sea-creatures are extinct, a live one turns up. A coelacanth (believed to have died out 70 million years ago) was caught in the Indian Ocean in 1939. More have been caught since – alive and flapping.

8.   Most of the Earth's ocean is in the southern half of the globe – but almost all of the fishing takes place in the north. The southern seas are almost undisturbed.

9.   Stories of sea-monsters have been told by groups of people all over the world. The people are separated by thousands of miles and thousands of years . . . yet the monsters are often similar. In northern Europe it was called the Kraken. When it surfaced it spread itself out over a distance of a mile and a half [2.4 km]. Sailors who

mistook it for an island would land on it, light their camp-fires then be left to swim for it when the monster dived. In Malagasy legend it is called The Lord of the Sea; the Ancient Greeks told of the monstrous Scylla.

10. Dolphins swimming in line look like a many-humped creature, as do swimming penguins. Other known creatures that have been mistaken for sea-monsters include seals, walruses, sea-lions, enormous conger eels, sea-cows (now believed extinct), whales, octopuses, and giant squid which can reach 20 metres and have been seen to fight whales!

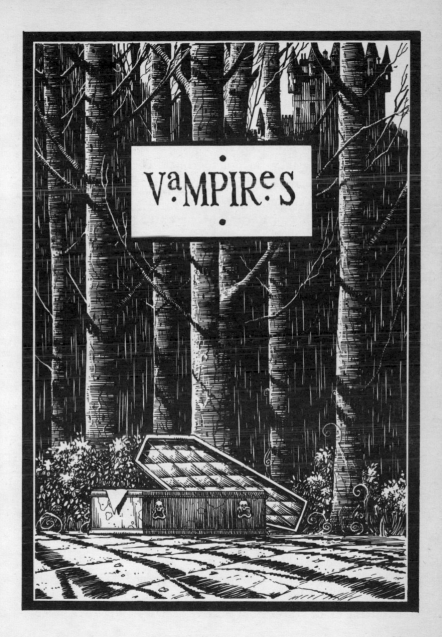

VAMPIRES

"Vampires issue forth from their graves in the night, attack people sleeping quietly in their beds, suck out all the blood from their bodies and destroy them."

John Heinrich Zopft, 1733

Vampires are the monsters of a nightmare. They are hard to recognize because they can look so human. They are hard to kill because they are already dead. They are hard to escape from because they can change into bats and fly after you. Yet, mixed in with the silly horror stories, there are true stories which are harder to explain. Two hundred years ago a very respectable group of lawyers, government officers and army officers reported on a series of strange goings-on in the Slavic regions and Baltic states of eastern Europe . . .

The Soldier's Story

The soldier stood to attention. He trembled as Colonel Linz shouted at him. "What are these stupid stories you have been spreading through the regiment, Private Koros?"

The soldier licked his lips. "Just the truth, sir!"

The commander sneered. "Truth? Truth! The truth is there are no such things as vampires."

"Yes, sir."

"What?"

"I mean no, sir. No such thing."

Colonel Linz strode up to the soldier and hissed, "You are a soldier in the Hungarian army – not some ignorant peasant."

"Yes, sir . . . I mean no, sir."

The colonel sighed and returned to his seat at the desk. "Stand at ease, Koros. Tell me what happened."

The soldier relaxed and ran a finger round his collar. "I'm not living in the army camp, sir. I've been sent out to live in the village – or rather, a farm on the edge of the village. A family called Bruck. They're nice, friendly people; treat me as one of the family."

The colonel just grunted.

"Then one night we were sitting down for dinner. We'd just started eating when the door swung open and this terrible smell drifted into the room. Made me feel quite sick. That's when the old man walked in. An ordinary bloke. Clothes a bit old fashioned, eyes a bit red. The smell seemed to be coming from *him*. There was nothing particularly strange about him. Like I said, he was just an old man. I thought it must have been a neighbour. But the family just froze like they'd seen a ghost."

"Yes," the colonel nodded. "Go on!"

"He didn't say a word. He just walked round the table till he came to the farmer, Mr Bruck, and sort of rested a hand on his shoulder. Then he walked out."

"What did the family do?" the colonel demanded.

Private Koros shrugged. "The daughters ran out of the room crying. Mrs Bruck just sat in her chair looking like she'd seen the devil himself. All she said was, "He'll be dead before sunrise.""

"And farmer Bruck? What did he do?"

The soldier shuddered. "He stood up, walked to his room and lay on the bed. Never got up again. The next day he was dead. Like Mrs Bruck said he'd be."

The colonel ran a hand over his iron-grey hair. "What exactly *did* Mrs Bruck say?"

"She *said* the old man was Mr Bruck's father . . . and he'd died ten years ago!"

Colonel Linz brought his fist crashing down. "Imagination! You never saw the old man."

"Yes, sir . . . I mean no, sir."

"What did your captain do when you told him the story?"

"Went to the graveyard and had the old man's body dug up, sir."

"Hah! There wouldn't be much more than a skeleton left after ten years," the colonel snorted.

Koros shook his head slowly. "The body was as fresh as if he'd died yesterday," he murmured.

"Imagination!" the commander barked. "And where did these stories about blood-drinking vampires come from? That's what I've been sent here to investigate. More fairy tales and lies, I suppose?"

"If you say so, sir," Koros said miserably. "But the villagers did tell us about another vampire in the region. He came back and killed three of his nieces in a fortnight. He was attacking his fourth niece when he was interrupted. The girl is dying. The villagers think the vampire escaped back to his grave."

Colonel Linz stood up. "Good! Then we can examine this grave right now. We shall put an end to these stories once and for all."

The soldier smiled. "Yes, sir."

"And to put your mind at rest, Koros, you can come and watch!"

The smile slid from the private's face. "Yes, sir," he said weakly.

And, to make it worse, he was given a spade and told to dig. Curious soldiers and frightened villagers gathered around as Koros started to unearth the coffin. The afternoon shadows had lengthened into evening by the time he had finished. At last the coffin was lifted clear and Colonel Linz stepped forward to take the spade from Koros. "Now!" he announced. "Let's have a look at this so-called vampire."

He swung the spade over his head and smashed the wooden

coffin lid into splinters. He stepped back as the foul smell hit him. The crowd gasped and shrank away at the sight that greeted them. The body was in perfect condition. Koros swore that he could see the heart still beating!

He snatched the spade from Colonel Linz and drove it deep into the heart of the vampire. A foul white liquid oozed out. Some of the onlookers thought they heard a hideous scream ... but in the confusion it was hard to tell. One thing was certain. The heart was no longer beating.

The body was destroyed with quick-lime and peace returned to the village. Strangely, from that moment, the fourth niece began at last to recover from her attack.

Colonel Linz and the official enquiry returned to Belgrade to make their report. And Private Koros lived to be an older and wiser man. "Vampires?" he used to say when the subject came up in the taverns around the flickering log fires. "Vampires?" he shuddered. "I once knew a man who said there's no such thing ..."

Vampire legends come from all over the world. They concern the 'undead' – the dead who rise again. Russian vampires are believed to have purple faces and are the human form of someone who, when alive, opposed the church.

In other countries vampires are easier to spot because of their curious features or disgusting habits. Bulgarian vampires have only one nostril; Bavarian vampires sleep with one eye open and thumbs linked; Brazilian vampires have their feet covered in a velvety fur while Albanian vampires can be seen wearing high heels. Chinese vampires draw their strength from the moon. Mexican vampires have no flesh on their skulls.

But most fearsome seem to be the vampires from the Rocky Mountains – they use their noses to suck their victims' blood out through the ears.

It would be wrong to think that vampire legends only exist in the distant past in some hidden corner of Europe. They persist in modern cities . . .

The Policeman's Story

I've been in the police force a long time now. In all those years I've seen some strange things – met some strange people. But the strangest thing – and the strangest person – was the case of the man who was killed by a vampire.

It's true . . . in a way. It happened back in January 1973. I was a young detective constable at the time, on duty in Stoke-on-Trent – that's in the English Midlands, as you may know.

Sounded like a routine case. I was sent to number Three, The Villas. The neighbours had reported that a seventy-year-old man had not been seen for a few days. Nothing strange about that. People often go missing. Usually we find them alive.

Mrs Ledger at number Two was a worried woman. "You reported your neighbour missing?" I said as she answered the door.

She nodded. I took out my notebook. "Mr Myiciura," she said.

"Er, could you spell that?" I asked.

"No. Can't you?" she replied.

I sighed. I made a guess at the spelling. "Funny name."

"Polish," she explained.

"And what makes you think he's missing?"

She shrugged herself into a worn old cardigan. "Milk bottles on the doorstep. I always see him to say hello to in the morning, and I haven't seen him for three days."

"That's Wednesday?" I noted. "Have you knocked at his door?"

"This afternoon," she said carefully. Her small eyes glittered in the light from the street lamp. "He doesn't like people knocking," she said in a hoarse whisper. "He's scared."

"Scared? Scared of what?"

Mrs Ledger leaned forward and her eyes flickered up and down the dark street. "Scared of things that come for you in the night."

I began to put my notebook away. It was clear I was dealing with a crank here. She shot out an arm and with a rough hand stopped me. "No! Honest. He came here after the last war with nothing. He ran away from the Germans. They killed his wife and family. Scared him witless it did!"

"And he thinks the Germans are still after him?" I asked.

She shook her thin head. "No. But he's a nervous man. He's had a hard life, and I wouldn't like to see anything happen to him. Poor old bloke. Poor, lonely old man," she sighed. Mrs Ledger looked as if she knew what it was to be poor and lonely. "Don't frighten him, eh?"

"I'll try," I promised, and walked the few steps to number Three.

I let the heavy iron knocker fall against the door. The knock boomed through the house like a tomb. An empty house with bare walls and floors. I'd seen a lot of houses like that in my time.

I waited as Mrs Ledger shivered in the shadow of her doorway. I tried the door. It was locked. I pushed it with my shoulder and the rotten old wood gave way. Another push and it splintered inwards. I found myself in a dark hallway that smelled of cabbage and old socks. I groped for a light switch, found a cold metal one and clicked it down. Nothing happened.

Mrs Ledger's voice came from the doorway. "He won't have electric in the house," she explained. "Too scared."

Luckily I carried a torch. I stepped towards the door on the right of the hall. My feet crunched in something powdery. The torch showed white crystals. Strung around the door were withered white bulbs.

The door to the room opened with a creak when I pushed it. My torch caught the pale, frightened face of the old man on the bed. He didn't move. Those wild, wide eyes didn't blink in the beam of the torch. I knew he was dead.

I closed the door softly and went off to call for assistance.

The first tests showed that he had choked to death. Choked on a pickled onion. There had to be an inquiry into the death – an inquest led by a coroner.

"A sad case," the coroner declared. "But people have been known to choke to death on their food before now." He turned to me. "Anything to add, constable?"

I swallowed hard. I could have let the case rest there. But I had decided to take a trip to the local public library before the inquest. Eventually I had come across a book called *The Natural History of the Vampire* that seemed to have the answer; that's how I knew what had scared old Myiciura to death.

I turned to the coroner. "Er, yes, sir," I said.

The coroner looked over the top of his glasses at me. "Well?"

I took a deep breath. "There were white crystals scattered all over his floor and over his bed. The lab report confirms that this was in fact salt. A packet of salt was found at the feet of the deceased."

The coroner looked a little blank but said, "Go on."

"The bulbs around the door proved to be garlic," I said.

"And what do you deduce from that, constable?" he asked.

"That Mr Myiciura was terribly afraid of vampires," I said.

The coroner blinked and the glasses almost fell off his nose. "Are you suggesting that he died as the result of a vampire attack? There were no marks on the body!"

"No, sir," I said quickly. "Just that he may have died of the *fear* of a vampire attack. In eastern Europe I believe people are convinced that such creatures exist."

The coroner sat back, took off his glasses and rubbed his eyes. "Very well. We will postpone this case for two weeks for further tests."

He left a stunned courtroom with some reporters, who were scribbling furiously about this ordinary case that had turned out to be a sensation.

But I was in the office when the new test results came in. Mr Myiciura *had* died of choking – but not on a pickled onion. He had choked on one of his own cloves of garlic.

The terrified man had slept with one in his mouth to keep away the vampires. As he fell asleep the garlic slid into his throat and choked him.

In a curious way, the vampires got him after all.

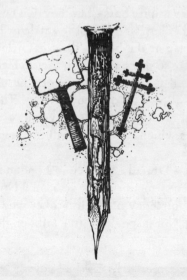

Vampires – FACT FILE

1.   The famous vampire Count Dracula is just a story written by Bram Stoker 100 years ago. That story is still popular today. Another story-book monster is almost forgotten today. He appeared in 1847, 50 years before Bram Stoker's *Dracula*. He was called *Varney the Vampire* and appeared in a serial story of 220 episodes. Varney died when he threw himself into a volcano.

2.   There *was* a man called Dracula who lived in eastern Europe – but he wasn't a vampire. Just a very cruel war-lord who terrorized the region. He was known as Vlad Dracula The Impaler through his vicious treatment of enemies and prisoners whom he impaled on sharp, pointed wooden stakes.

3.   There *are* vampire bats – but they don't usually suck human blood. They find sleeping cattle or horses, nip the skin and lap at the blood like a cat drinking milk. Their teeth are so sharp that their victim feels nothing. A substance in their saliva prevents the blood from clotting and allows it to keep flowing. Their blood-drinking will rarely kill – but they can carry diseases such as rabies which eventually kill the victim.

4.   There is a Dracula Society in London and one in California. They meet once a year on 8 November to celebrate the birthday of Bram Stoker who wrote the book *Dracula*. Guest speakers give talks on the vampire legends.

5.   Traditionally people believe that garlic and salt will keep vampires away and even poison them. Sprinkling chalk and holy water is also supposed to be effective. But the only sure way to kill a vampire is to force a wooden or iron stake through its heart. Vampires have been reported to scream when this is done. Some are even supposed to cry. Those who want to be certain the vampire is dead will cut off the head and have the body burned.

6.   Traditionally people believe that they can protect themselves from vampires by making the sign of the cross. Vampires don't like the Church, and the Church doesn't like vampires. The churches of eastern Europe used to claim that anyone leading a wicked life could become a vampire. They also believed that a victim could not be forced to enter the vampire's lair. An invitation had to be offered by free choice if the vampire was to succeed.

7.   Vampire legends go back many thousands of years to Greek, Roman and Hebrew mythology. But the strongest legends centre around Transylvania in Romania, eastern Europe. The Romanians have a popular tourist industry based on the stories; they have opened a *Castle Dracula* hotel with tape-recorded wolves howling as visitors drive towards it.

8.   Legends say that a vampire can be a man or a woman. The victim of a vampire is said to become a vampire in turn. Eating the earth from the vampire's grave can be a cure, however.

9.   In the 17th and 18th centuries body-snatchers stole corpses from graves and sold them to doctors for medical experiments. The body-snatchers left the graves empty. Ignorant and frightened people thought that the corpses had found their own way out.

10.   Those who believe in vampires explain their undead state in two ways: vampires are evil spirits that take over corpses and use them; vampires are the spirits of dead people who were too wicked to be allowed into the after-life – they have to return to their old body to find a 'home'.

WEREWOLVES

Even he who is pure of heart
And says his prayers by night
May become a wolf when the wolfbane blooms
And the moon is full and bright.
Traditional European proverb

Werewolf stories are among the oldest horror stories in the world. They probably began with legends of Norse gods who had powers to change themselves into animals – including wolves. The stories were given extra power by country people who lived in fear of real wolves; then there were actual cases of mentally ill people who believed they were animals and tried to eat raw flesh to prove it.

A disease of the body called Hypertrichosis can cause the body and entire face to be covered in hair. This too could have led ignorant people to believe that the sufferer was infected by a werewolf.

No matter how impossible it seems for a human to change shape some people will always believe in werewolves. People like the Reverend Montague Summers, a well-known 19th century writer on the supernatural. He described an encounter which he said happened in Wales in 1888 . . .

Professor Richard Eldon was pleased with himself. He stood at the door of the mountain cottage and breathed the clear Merionethshire air. "Wonderful, Avril!" he cried to his wife. "Didn't I tell you I'd give you the best holiday you've ever had?"

Avril Eldon had spent an hour unpacking their cases. She had lit the fire in the stove and begun to cook an evening meal.

Her husband had spent that hour on the porch of the cottage smoking his pipe and staring at the mountains shimmering in the sun. "Wonderful views . . . and so peaceful. Nothing can disturb us here. We can really relax."

The woman staggered into the cottage with an armful of logs and said pointedly, "Can you, dear?"

Her husband didn't seem to notice the edge in her voice. "Ye-es. We can walk up those mountains tomorrow," he promised.

Avril pushed a wisp of hair from her brow and winced. "Oh, good," she said flatly. "First you could help me make the beds. The linen's in the cupboard and it needs taking out now. It'll have to be aired before we sleep in it tonight."

The professor pulled a large watch out of his waistcoat pocket. "Hmm. If I'm going to get any fishing in today I'll have to set off now," he sighed and turned to pick up his fishing basket. "You'll manage."

His wife opened her mouth to object but he went on, "That seems fair enough to me. You make the beds while I catch our supper . . . I'll be back before sunset," he promised as he marched down the hillside.

The professor returned at sunset, just as he'd promised, but without the fish he'd said he'd bring.

"Sorry, my love," he sighed. "There don't seem to be any fish in that lake – or, if there are, then something's scaring them away."

"Just as well I made a shepherd's pie, then," his wife sniffed.

He dropped his fishing basket on the white table-cloth and Avril reached forward quickly to lift it off. "That's clean!" she cried. Then, feeling the weight of the basket, she added, "Well, you must have caught something."

The professor blinked. "What? Oh, yes. Almost forgot. I found a fascinating thing down by the lake . . . most unusual."

He opened the wicker basket and took out a huge skull. Avril wasn't usually upset at the sight of bones. But something about this skull disgusted her. "What on earth is it?"

Her husband shrugged. "Thought we'd take it back to the college at the end of the holiday. One of the chaps in the science department might tell us. It's not a sheep – too big."

"And those huge teeth belong to a meat-eater," his wife added. "Some sort of dog?"

"I've never seen a dog that big. That's why it's so exciting. I thought it could be prehistoric," the man said proudly. "Just pop it on that shelf for now. We'll look at it again after supper."

But after supper the professor had other plans. "The pub?" his wife groaned. "You're going to the pub down in the village and leaving me here alone?"

The man shrugged. "Tore my trousers on some bushes down by the lake. Thought you could darn them for me. It'll keep you occupied. See you later. Shouldn't be more than a couple of hours," he promised as he vanished through the door.

Avril Eldon lit one of the oil-lamps in the cottage and took out her sewing basket. As she bent over her mending she noticed that the room was growing brighter. Looking up she saw the moon rising over the mountains and flooding through the window. The mountains were black and deserted and silent.

A soft snuffling sound was the first hint that she was not alone. She looked up sharply. The empty eyes of the skull stared down at her from the shelf. Then there was a sharp scraping at the door as if some dog was asking to come in.

Avril put down her needle and walked over to check that the door was fastened tight. There was a small window beside the door. As she reached it a shadow blotted out the moonlight. The huge face of an enormous dog was peering in at her with great, glowing eyes.

The eyes were fixed on her, willing her to open the door. But she knew she had to fight them and forced her own eyes shut, blindly finding the beam that barred the door.

She leaned with her back to the door and saw those eyes in her mind. Intelligent eyes . . . human eyes. And weren't those paws on the sill more like human hands?

Suddenly she remembered the front door. Racing through the house she reached the bolts just as the latch rattled. She heard the creature panting hungrily. It snarled when the door refused to give and growled as it walked around the house looking for another way in.

The woman sank, trembling, to the floor and pressed her back to the door, her legs too weak to move. Time and again the beast barged and bumped against the door. Then Avril did something she hadn't done for years. She prayed. She said every prayer she could remember from her days in Sunday School and a few that she made up on the spot. When she stopped mumbling the Lord's Prayer for the last time she was surprised to find that the noises had gone.

She rose weakly to her feet and laughed at her own nervous state. "Just a dog," she muttered. "Just a dog."

Then she froze as the gravel outside the door rattled and the latch clattered.

Thump! Thump! Thump! The door shook.

Then a voice. A human voice. A voice she hardly recognized. "Avril! Open the door, woman! Avril!"

Her trembling hands pulled back the bolts and tugged the door open. She dragged her husband inside and quickly locked them in again.

The professor blinked. "What's wrong, my dear? You look as if you've seen a ghost!"

Avril shook her head slowly. "No. Something much, much

worse than any ghost." And she told her husband about the ghastly visitor.

Professor Eldon frowned. "That ties up with something the villagers told me in the pub. Some story about that lake being haunted by a man-wolf. What was it they called it? Yes. A werewolf. Just as well I came prepared for some shooting," he said grimly as he slid a rifle out of its leather case. He checked that it was loaded and sat at the table staring out into the night.

Hours passed. The couple kept up their unblinking watch. Then as the moon sank, and even the owls had returned to their nests, the face of the wolf with the eyes of a man appeared at the window. Professor Eldon snatched his gun and ran to the door. The wolf saw the movement and fled ahead of him.

Even in the darkness of that mountain night the creature had its own greenish, ghoulish glow. The man followed the beast down the path to the lake.

The werewolf stopped at the edge of the lake, turned and looked back with its hot-coal eyes. As the professor raised the rifle to fire, the creature howled and plunged itself into the lake.

But as it hit the water it disappeared without a splash, without a ripple.

The man staggered with exhaustion towards the cottage. His wife was standing behind him. In her hands she held the ivory skull.

Without a word he nodded, took it from her hands and walked to the edge of the water. He threw it as far into the lake as he could. Putting his arm around his wife's shoulder he walked back to the cottage.

The sunrise came.

The werewolf was never seen again.

Peace returned to the lake. But peace never returned to the Eldons. The monster lived on in their minds and troubled their dreams for ever after.

Monster Werewolf – FACT FILE

1. A werewolf is said to be rather like a vampire when they are both in human form. They have small, pointed ears, hair on the palms of their clawed hands and eyebrows that meet in the middle. The werewolf, however, has the ring finger of each hand a little longer than the middle finger – in humans and vampires the middle finger is longer.

2. Superstitious people believe that if you sleep outdoors when a full moon falls on a Friday, then you may turn into a werewolf. Eating the plant wolfbane can have this effect too.

3. Human shape-changers can take many forms depending on where in the world they are: in Africa people believed in wereleopards, in India weretigers, in Scandinavia, werebears.

4. Wereanimal stories are often linked with stories of witchcraft. The theory was that witches could turn themselves into animals whenever they wanted. The animal was often a hare, because it could sprint away from witch-hunters, but was often a cat or a toad. In the 1500s the wolf was added to the list of witch forms.

5. If attacked by a werewolf then, Canadians say, a good defence is to speak the name of Christ. The French recommend taking three drops of the wolf's blood. The

most famous method, favoured by film-makers, is to take the silver from a church crucifix, mould it into the shape of a bullet and shoot the werewolf.

6.   Werewolves are believed to grow hair *inside* their bodies. Sadly one suspect died in Italy in 1541 when his accusers tried to prove this by cutting him open. He was innocent of course – but that was no comfort to the dead man's family.

7.   A *Lycanthrope* is a mentally-ill person who believes he has taken the form of a wolf. In 1589 Peter Stump of Cologne, Germany, confessed to changing himself magically into a wolf. That is unlikely, but what is certain is that he killed many human and animal victims while overcome by the illness.

8.   A twelfth–century poem tells of a knight who was a werewolf three days of the week but had no savage habits. His unfaithful wife had a lover; the lover stole the knight's clothes while he was in werewolf shape. Without his clothes the werewolf could not regain his human form and return to being a knight.

9.   If a werewolf is wounded in its wolf form then its human form will suffer a similar wound. For example, cut off the wolf's paw and it becomes a man with a missing hand. This is known as *wound-doubling*.

10.   King John of England was not only unpopular, he was also supposed to be a werewolf. After his death his body could not rest in holy ground; a Norman manuscript says that some monks heard him moving underground so they dug him up and reburied him outside holy ground.